PERCY THE MECHANICAL MAN

THE FIRST

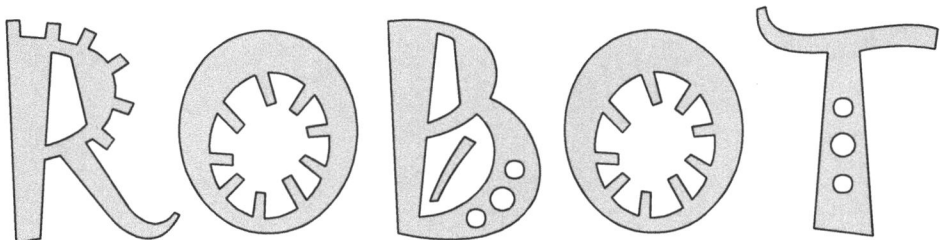

OF COMICS

By Harry Cornell Greening

Introduction by Kevin Scott Collier

PERCY THE MECHANICAL MAN
THE FIRST ROBOT OF COMICS

By Harry Cornell Greening

Introduction by Kevin Scott Collier

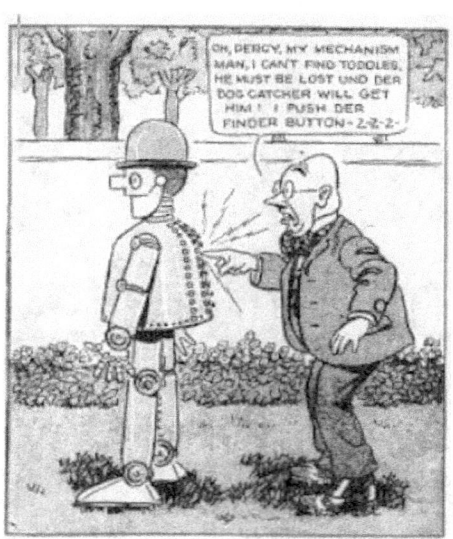

Percy and Creator Harry Cornell Greening

By Kevin Scott Collier

Cartoonist Harry Cornell Greening was born in 1876 in Titusville, Pennsylvania. He took an interest in art at an early age, and imagining a career in illustration, enrolled at the Art Students League of New York in 1896, where he studied drawing.

That same year, Greening freelanced illustrations, scoring his first sales with the *New York Herald* newspaper, *Life* magazine, and *Truth* magazines.

In 1898, Greening was hired by the Hearst organization, where his job as an artist involved producing comic strips and single-panel news and editorial cartoons.

In 1902, Greening created his first published comic strip series, *Si Swapper*, for the *New York Herald*. The comic was about a trader.

Subsequently, Greening became a contributor to such periodicals as *Puck, Judge, Harper's,* and *Scribner's.* He originated the comic series *Prince Red Feather,* for the children's magazine *St. Nicholas,* during this period, as well.

Greening created several comic strip series for the *New York Herald*, including *Percy the Mechanical Man*, in 1911, and *Fritz von Blitz*, and *Prince Errant*.

During World War I, Greening worked as an artist for the American Expeditionary Forces.

In the 1920's, Greening hooked up with the McClure Syndicate, which distributed a comic strip he had created, titled *Eb and Flo*. He also was a frequent contributor to the *Los Angeles Illustrated Daily News*.

Harry C. Greening lived with his parents in Titusville and New Jersey for over half of

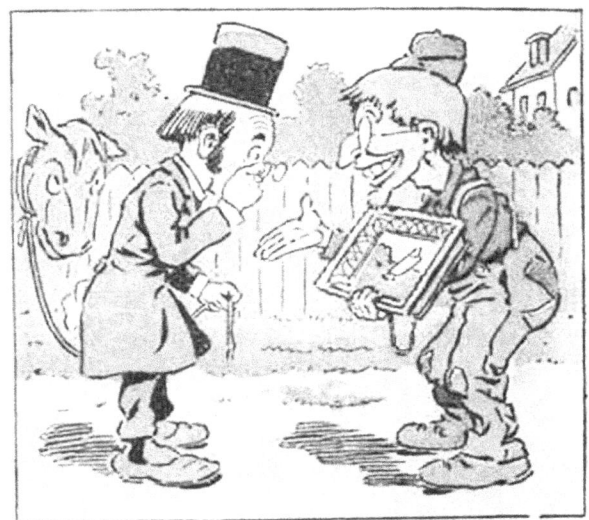

"NOW, DOMMINIE, THIS IS AN OLE MASTER; BUT IF YOU INSIST ON MY SWAPPIN' FER THET SPAVINED MARE, ALL O. K."

Si Swapper comic strip.

his life, moving out on his own to Los Angeles by 1930, continuing his work as a newspaper cartoonist. Greening also authored a fairy tale book, *The Wishbone Man*, published by Century Co., in 1924. Greening also invented toys for children.

Harry Cornell Greening died in 1949 from complications of diabetes. He was 73.

History has recognized Greening's automaton comic strip as introducing a robot in a starring role into the entertainment world. A single animated cartoon, in 1916, added to the popularity.

Harry C. Greening's character *Percy*, the "mechanism man," made his comics debut on October 1, 1911. The absent-minded robot servant, appearing every Sunday in a full-page color tale, quickly caught on with readers.

Percy's creator, a professor possessing a rich German dialect, was said to be brilliant but had little common sense. He and the

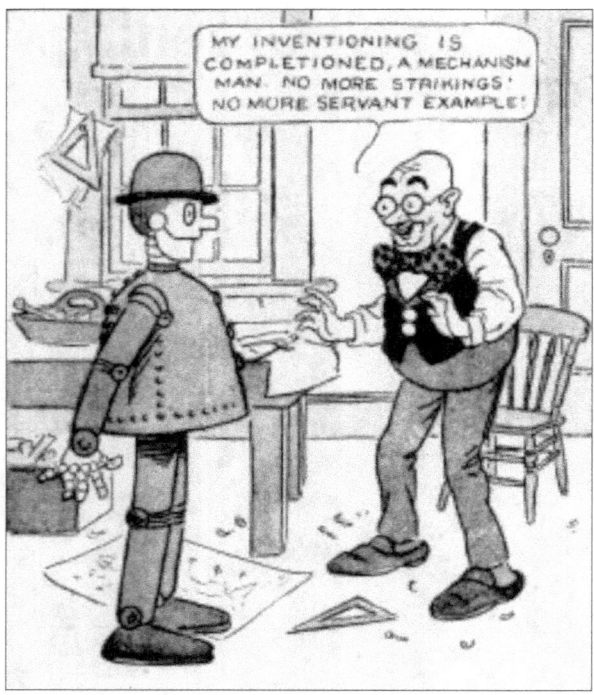

Panel from the first *Percy* comic strip, 1911.

robot were a disaster waiting to happen.

Percy could be pre-programmed to do tasks by pressing any number of buttons on his back. The process needed no tech degree. Thus, anyone pressing the buttons could set Percy in motion. Pushing the wrong buttons also resulted in undesired animated antics.

The banner at the top of the weekly comic also amused, as it frequently featured a gag drawing associated with the strip below.

Hearst distributed *Percy*, which was published in the *New York Herald*, *Washington Star*, and many other daily newspapers across the nation.

Generally, folks appreciated the robot, who was a good worker, but were keenly aware that the mechanical man "had no brains." Thus, early in the series run, Greening added a subtitle. The series became known as *Percy Brains He Has Nix*, on December 10, 1911.

The phrase, "brains he has nix," became a national catchword quickly. The sentence even made it into academic and trade journals, such as *The Michigan State Medical Journal* in June 1912, and the *Leather Worker's Journal* in July 1914.

Greening's introduction of a robot into the comics world wasn't new. It had been done previously, but never as a series. Thus, Percy earns the distinction of being the first syndicated comic strip that starred a mechanical man or robot.

It wasn't the first time a robot had been created for entertainment purposes.

According to sources, British writer and humorist, Jerome J. Jerome, introduced an automaton dancing partner in his novel *The Dancing Partner*, published in 1893. The same year M. L. Campbell presented a tale featuring the Automatic Maid of All Work. It appeared in the July issue of *Canadian Magazine*. A few years later, Elizabeth Bellamy created *Ely's Automatic Housemaid*, which was published in *The Black Cat* fiction stories magazine.

Early vaudeville productions occasionally introduced mechanical men, which were actors in creative-looking costumes appearing in traveling roadshows. Rarely were any of the devices actual machines.

Once Greening's *Percy* comic strip series gained popularity, copycats, intentional or coincidental, began to pop up in a variety of entertainment media.

One clear theft occurred in 1912, when showman John P. Harris arranged an exhibition at a theatre featuring "Percy," a mechanical man seven feet in height, electrically operated. Harris, an amusement company owner, presented a robot that responded to push buttons in his back. It was claimed the automaton could ride a bicycle, write on a blackboard and perform numerous tasks.

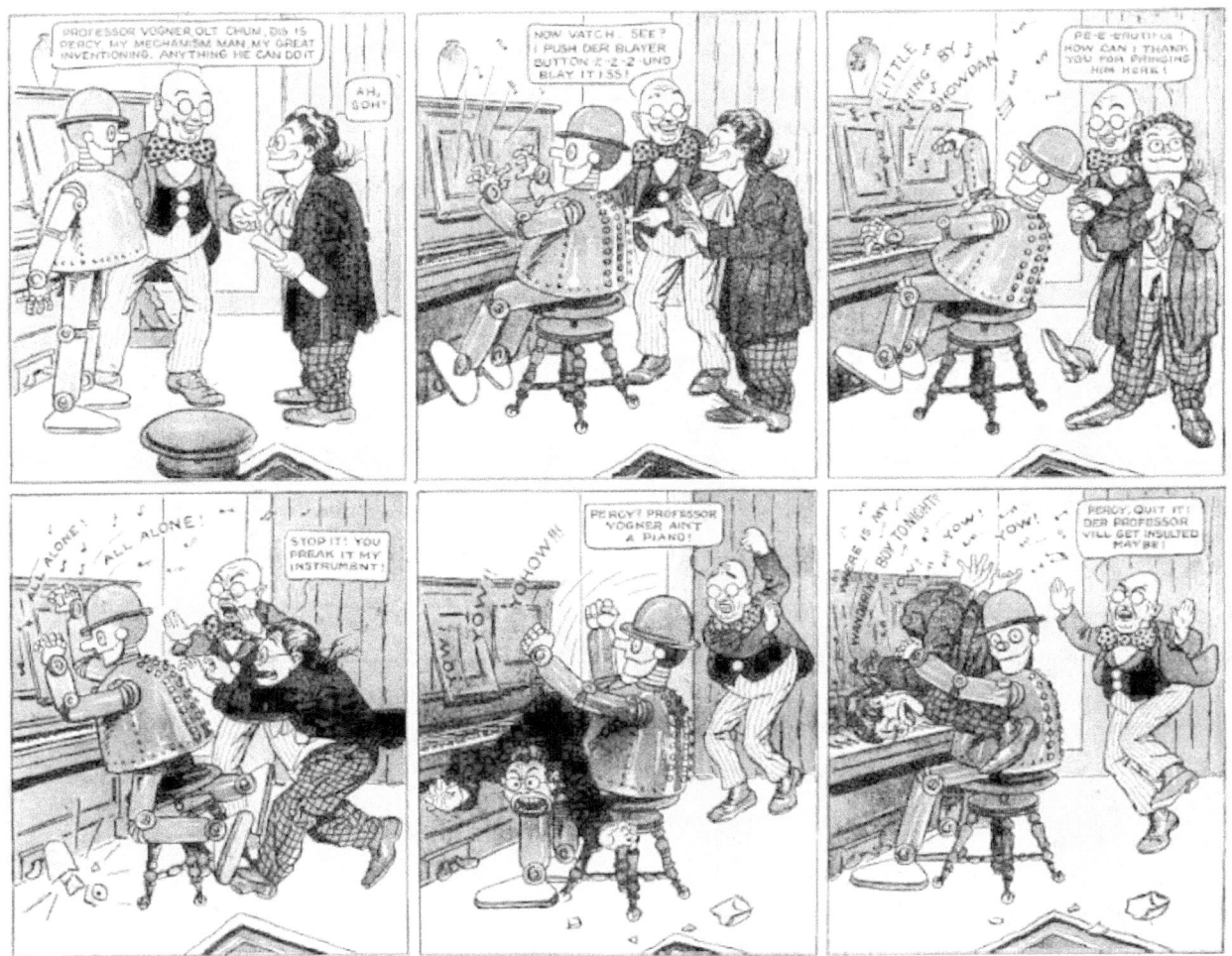

Panels from a *Percy* comic strip, by Greening, 1911.

The show ran briefly at Pittsburgh's Harris Theater, which he owned.

Roy Bowman also stole Greening's creation for personal benefit, for a stage production originating in Galveston, Texas. Reported in the February 23, 1912 edition of *The Galveston Daily News*, "Percy, the mechanical man," featured Bowman dressed in a brilliant costume, assisted by H. J. Schutje, who acted in the role of the professor."

The Lebanon Daily News speculated on automatons in the future, stating in an October 1912 issue, "Our children may live to see Percy, the mechanical man doing the work that in less advanced days was done by creatures of flesh and blood."

Percy the Mechanical Man comic strip ended on January 13, 1913. Harry C. Greening continued what would be a long career in newspaper cartooning.

Greening occasionally dusted Percy off and plunked him inside of his subsequent comic strips, appearing as a cameo. The image of the mechanical man always brought smiles and positive response.

In the fall of 1916, *Bray Studios*, a leading animation film company announced it had expanded its staff and was acquiring new content for cartoons.

"The enlargement of staff of cartoonists at

the Bray Studios will enable the producers to give a greater variety of subjects," *Motion Picture World* reported on September 9.

The expanded staff included nine cartoonists, thirty assistant artists, and four camera operators. The company had also patented a special animation method invented by studio founder, John Randolph Bray, to increase output. It made it possible for the company to create animated cartoons in half the time previously achieved.

The process produced copies of scene backgrounds, requiring artists only to draw principal people and objects that required movement.

John Bray approached Harry C. Greening that fall, and the two agreed to create an animated cartoon featuring *Percy the Mechanical Man*.

The film, lost to time, provided a name for the robot's inventor, Herr Professor Doodlepoodle, N. U. T.

Greening would illustrate the cartoon, with assistance from staff artists working from character model sheets.

In a press release, Bray wrote that Percy's "first job is as a window dresser in a department store," in the film. Bray also announced Percy "will be in a series form," indicating the intention was for the production of more than one cartoon.

"Percy is hired out to the manager [of the department store] by the professor, who goes on his way dreaming of immense profits," Bray said. "The trouble with the mechanical man is that he insists on dressing everyone. He doesn't stop at the windows. He disrobes the manager and places feminine garb upon him and then he creates havoc among all the customers in the store."

The film, titled *Percy the Mechanical Man: Brains He Has Nix*, was released into

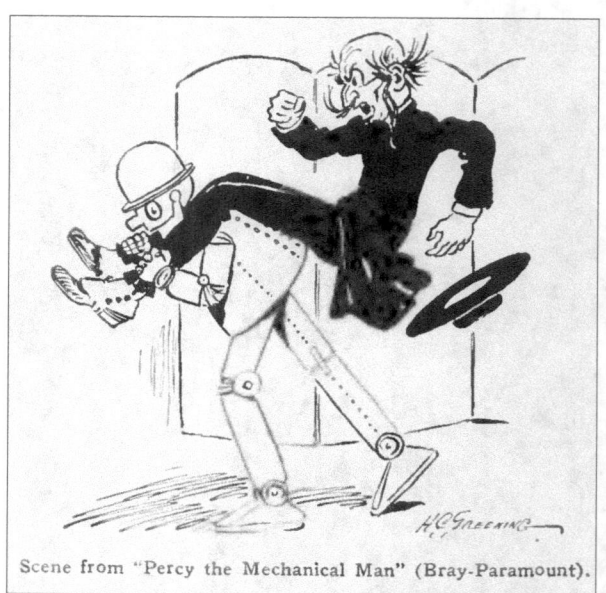

Scene from "Percy the Mechanical Man" (Bray-Paramount).

Illustration by Greening for the Bray cartoon, 1916.

theaters on December 21 that year.

The only glimpse of the complete content of the cartoon is revealed in a review published in *Moving Picture World*, published days after the film's release, on December 23, 1916.

The review read:

"Professor Doodlepoodle, N. U. T., famed in both hemispheres—and New Jersey, after many years of earnest effort and—short rations and long expectations, finally succeeds in completing the mechanical man, that is more than human. This contrivance he christened 'Percy.'

"I don't know why he named it Percy, nor does the Professor. He says that it looks as if its name were Percy, and he'll leave it up to anyone if it doesn't.

"The sudden climax of his hopes and efforts was almost too much for the gentle Professor. He grasps the child of his skill in both arms, inadvertently pushing many buttons at once. *Wow! It works by means of buttons.* By pushing the 'Walker Button' Percy is made to walk; by shoving the 'Dishwasher Button' Percy is made to wash dishes. But the result of pressing a number of buttons, as did the Professor when he impulsively threw his arms about his invention, was unknown—for a second, or a small fraction thereof. Then there was a disturbance commonly known as a 'rough house'—it is the only term properly descriptive.

"The Professor flies through the roof, interrupting an innocent cat who has had her eye on a sparrow luncheon. On landing he hits the roof, then Percy. As he gazes around the wreck of the shop, he realizes that he is ruined. But he has Percy! Percy shall recoup the Professor's fortune! He will hire him out at a good salary, for Percy can do anything a man can do—and most of the things a woman can.

"They pass down a street, and a sign in a dry goods emporium arrests the attention of the Professor: 'Window Dresser Wanted.' Percy is taken inside and introduced to the manager of the store. The manager wishes a demonstration and suggests that Percy dress a dummy to prove himself fitted for the job. Percy picks up the dummy, carries it behind the screen, and emerges with the fully and tastefully dressed figure. He is a success! He is hired on the spot and the Professor leaves—with the Dresser Button still working.

"Percy gives a few spasmodic starts, and grabs the store manager, carrying him behind the screen! Soon articles of personal wear appear from the back of the screen, then an enraged and outraged manager appears. That starts the fun—the rest is a riot. Lady customers are dressed in the latest styles for men; even the clergy is not exempt.

"When you see the Reverend Fiddle, D. D., beating it through the various depart-

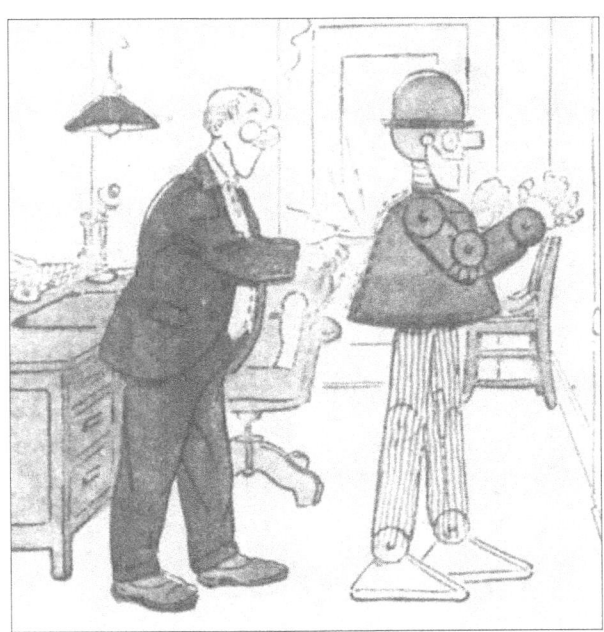

The return of *Percy* in newspapers, 1919-1920.

ments dressed in—but we won't give it away, we've said more than we should now."

The animated cartoon was well received.

From 1918-1919, Greening presented a version of *Percy* in his comic strip, *Fritz von Blitz*, starring a mechanical man.

Greening resurrected *Percy* in a comic strip for a brief period afterward. It reappeared first under the title *Percy* on March 2, 1919, then Greening developed a storyline putting the robot in show business, renaming it *Percy in Stageland*. The comic last appeared on March 28, 1920.

Ron Goulart, author of *The Funnies: 100 Years of American Comic Strips*, called Percy the "first robot to star in a Sunday page of his own."

Percy the Mechanical Man, in its time, became the symbol for robots in America. His popularity influenced real efforts to construct a mechanical man. Often in such projects the automaton was named "Percy."

The complete 1911-1913 *Percy* comic strip series follows, all 68 editions.

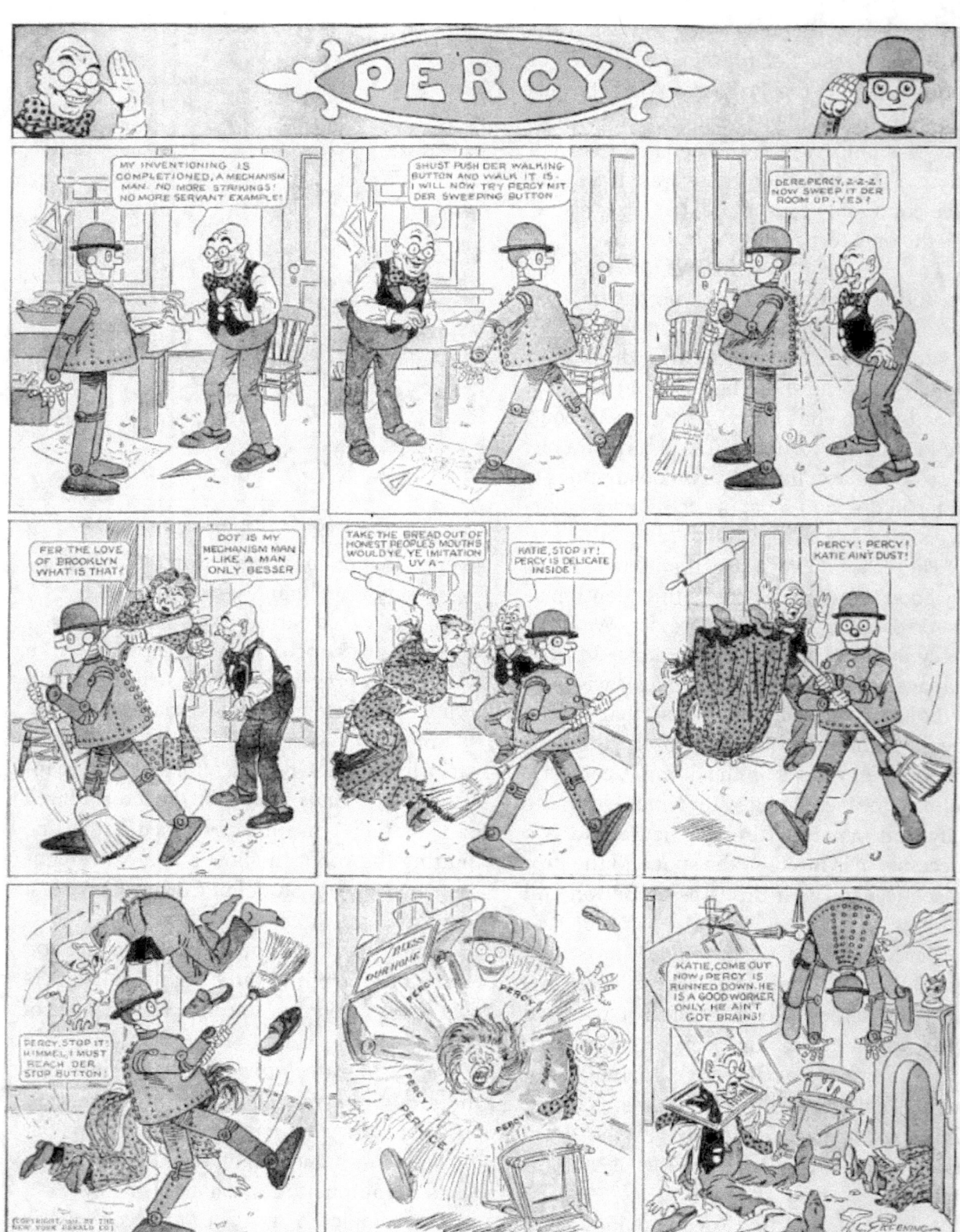

Percy: Brains He Has Nix by Harry Cornell Greening / Comic Strip #1 / Published in the Washington Evening Star October 1, 1911

8

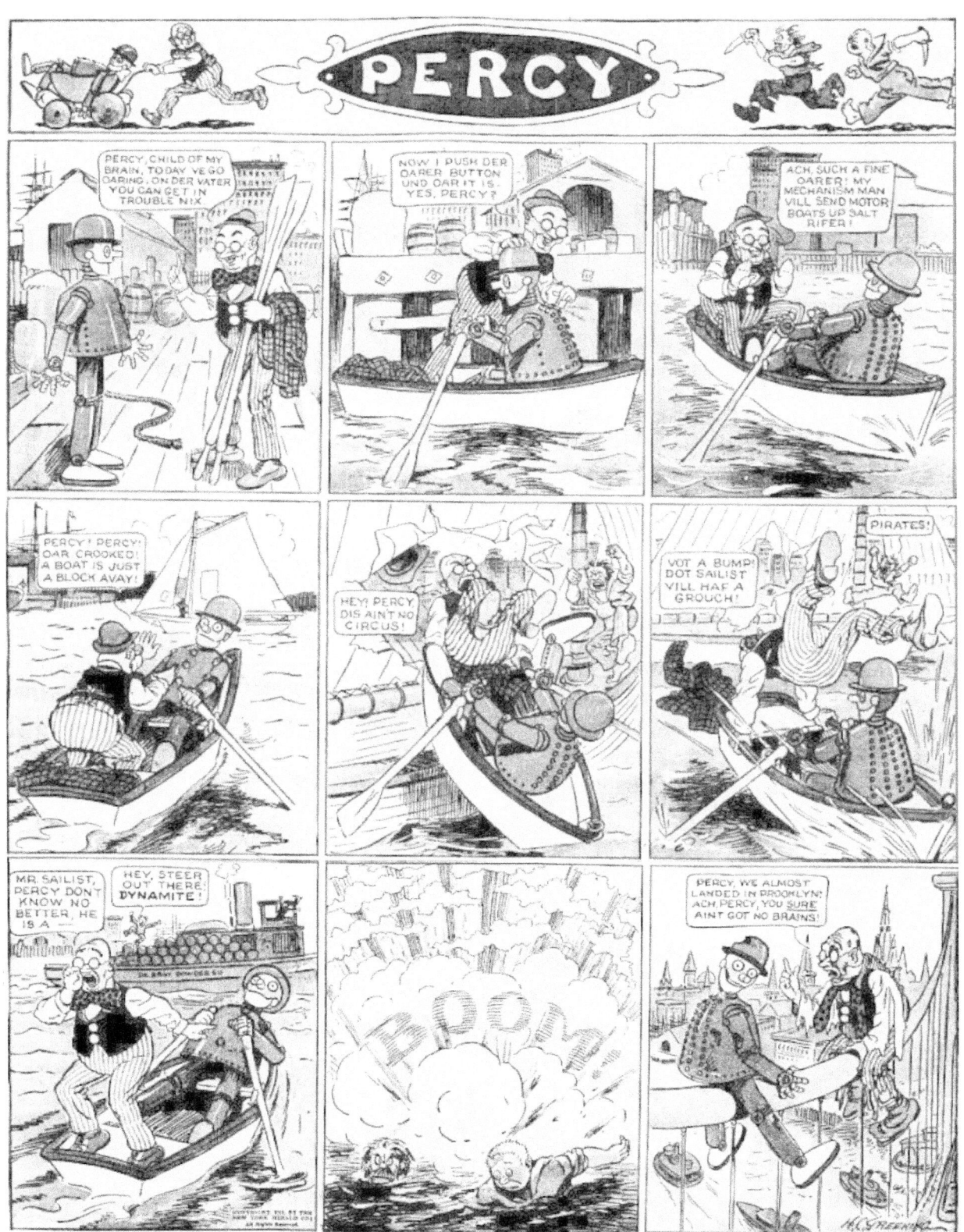

Percy: Brains He Has Nix by Harry Cornell Greening / Comic Strip #2 / Published in the Washington Evening Star October 8, 1911

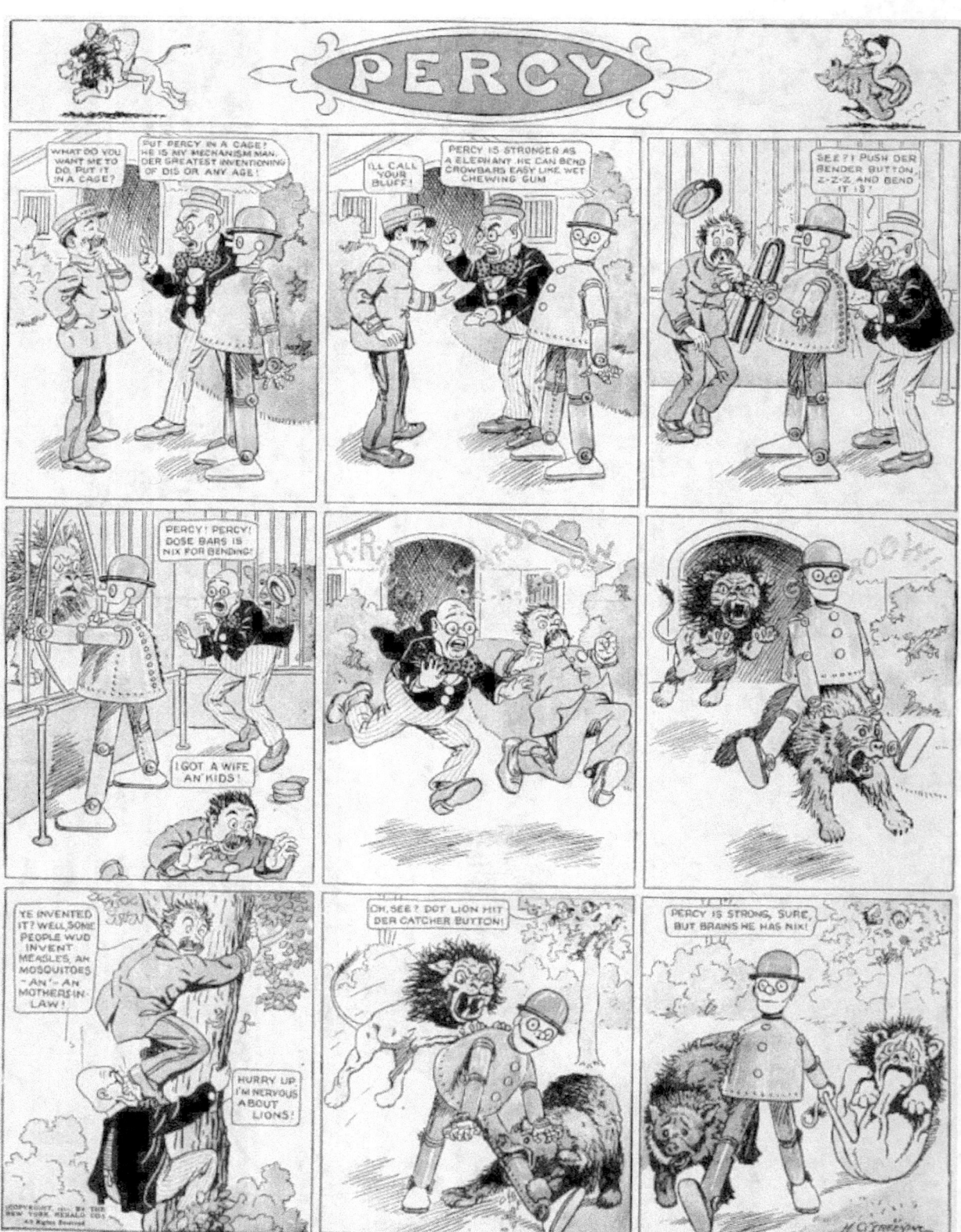

Percy: Brains He Has Nix by Harry Cornell Greening / Comic Strip #3 / Published in the Washington Evening Star October 15, 1911

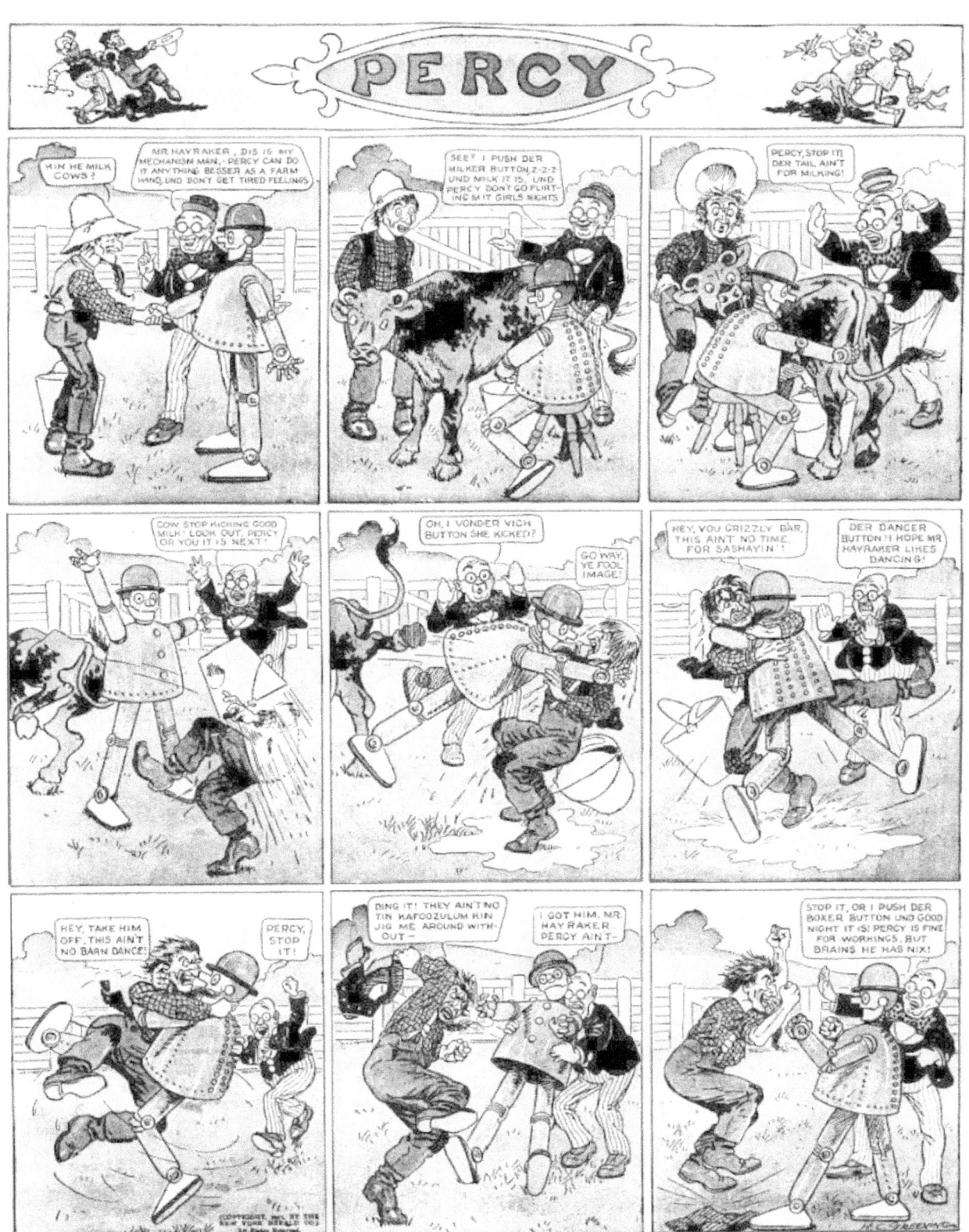

Percy: Brains He Has Nix by Harry Cornell Greening / Comic Strip #4 / Published in the Washington Evening Star October 22, 1911

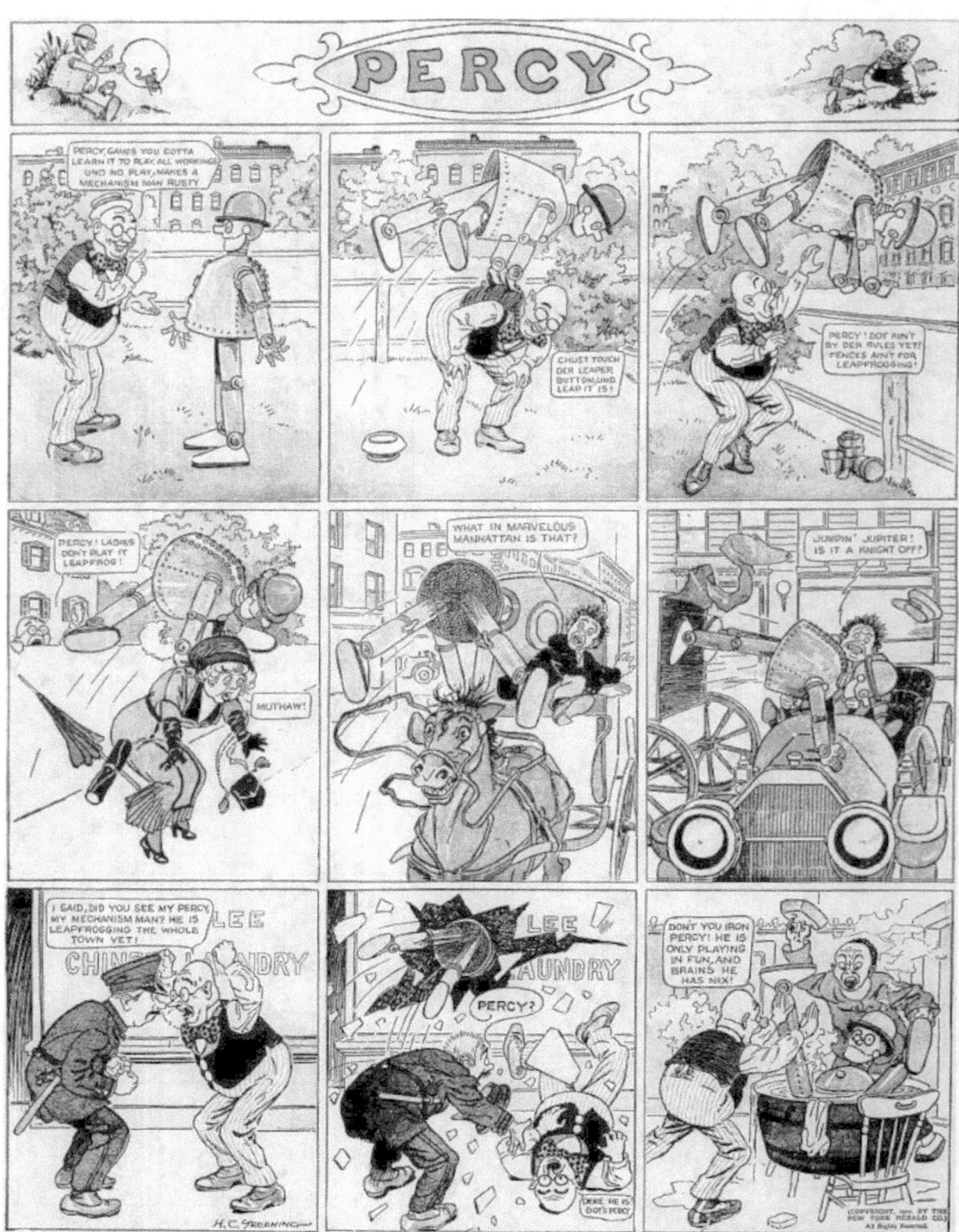

Percy: Brains He Has Nix by Harry Cornell Greening / Comic Strip #5 / Published in the Washington Evening Star October 29, 1911

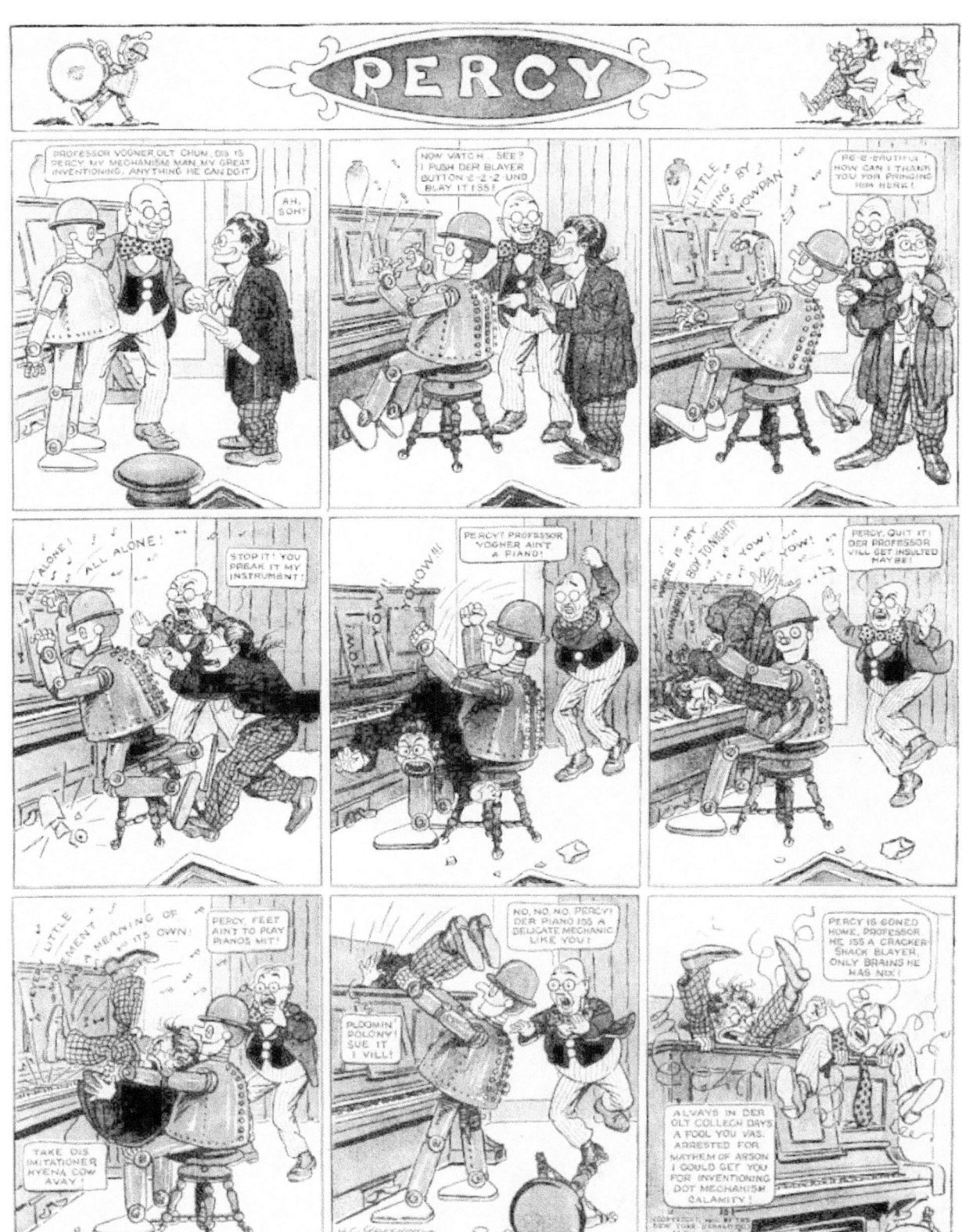

Percy: Brains He Has Nix by Harry Cornell Greening / Comic Strip #6 / Published in the Washington Evening Star November 5, 1911

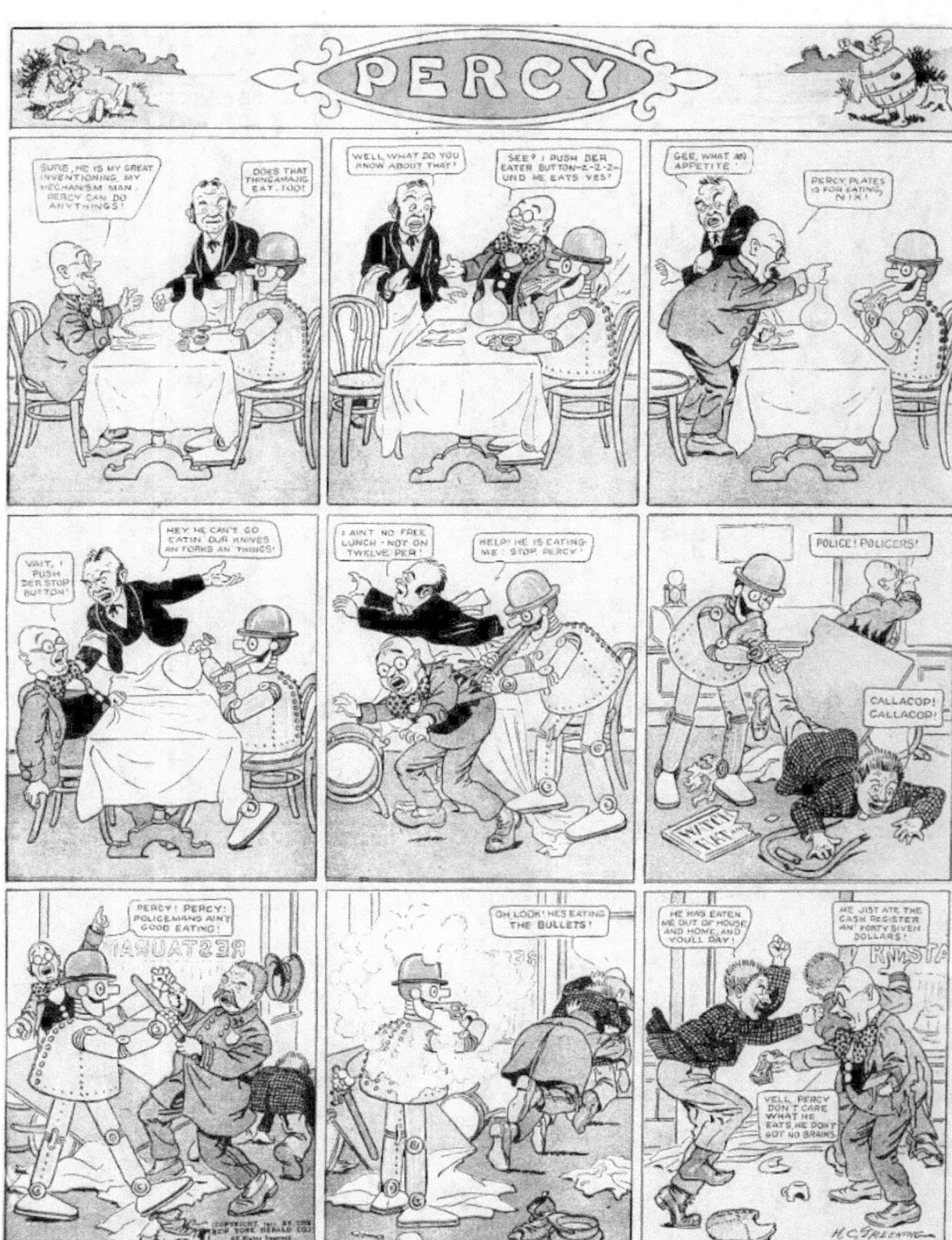

Percy: Brains He Has Nix by Harry Cornell Greening / Comic Strip #7 / Published in the Washington Evening Star November 12, 1911

14

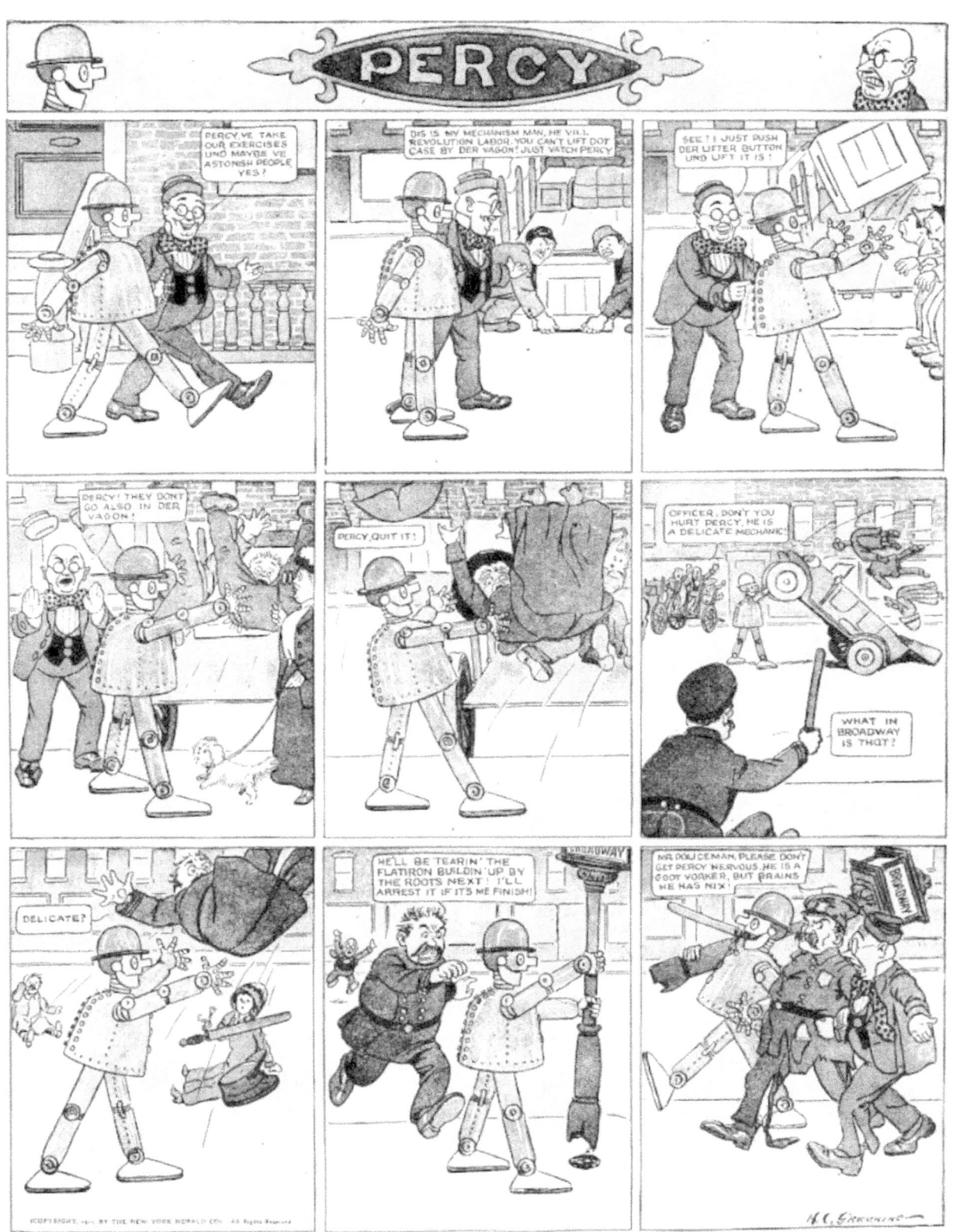

Percy: Brains He Has Nix by Harry Cornell Greening / Comic Strip #8 / Published in the Washington Evening Star November 19, 1911

15

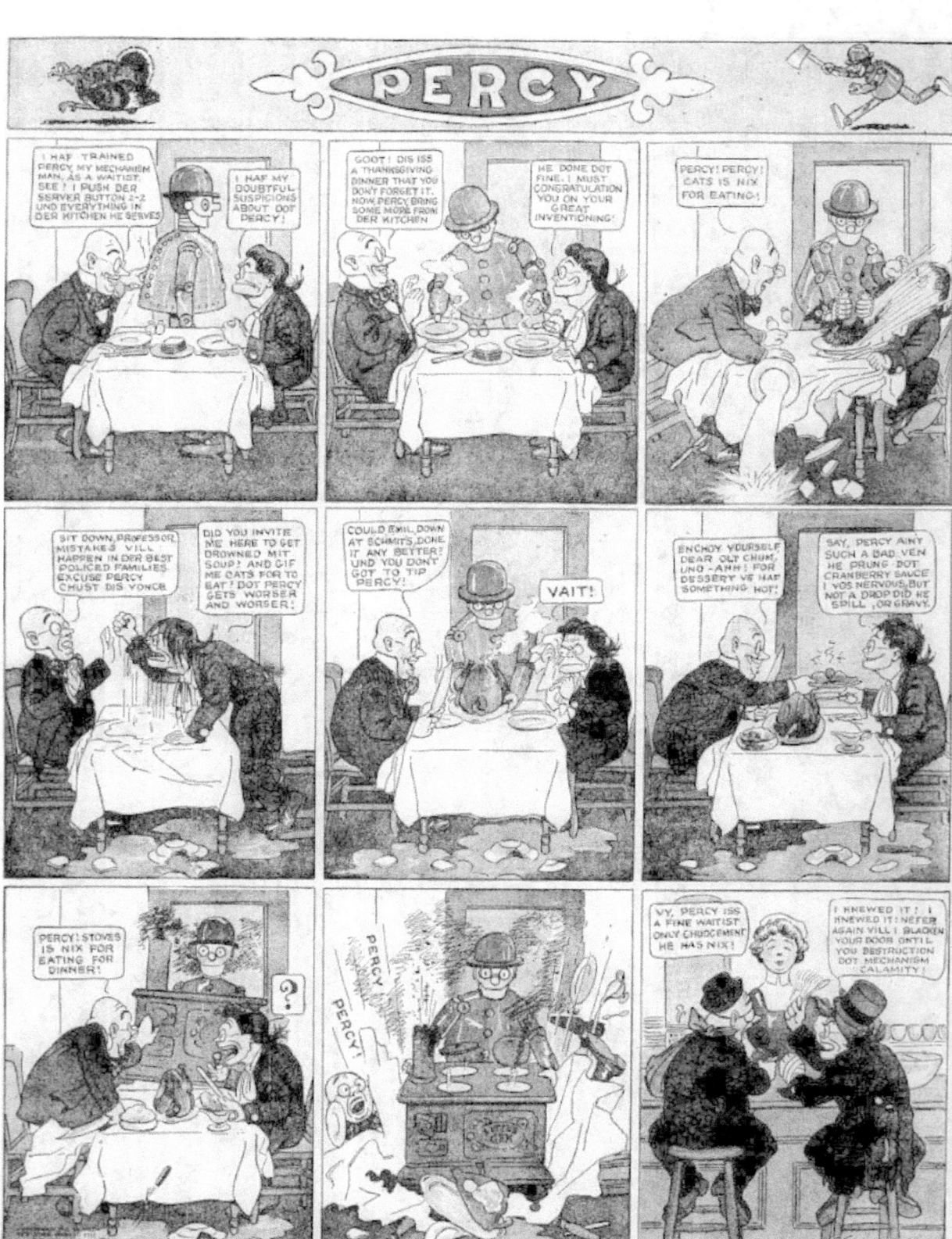

Percy: Brains He Has Nix by Harry Cornell Greening / Comic Strip #9 / Published in the Washington Evening Star November 26, 1911

16

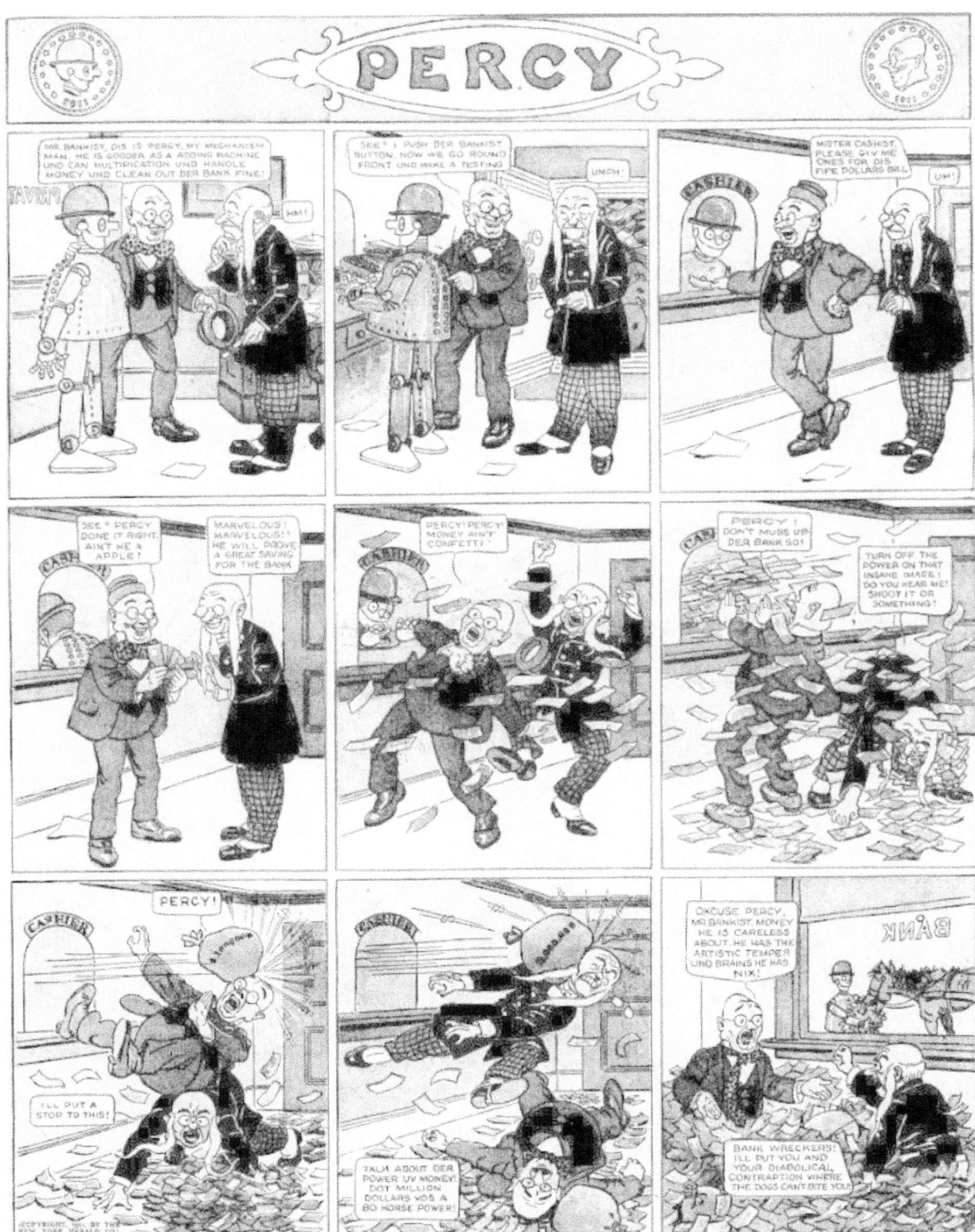

Percy: Brains He Has Nix by Harry Cornell Greening / Comic Strip #10 / Published in the Washington Evening Star December 3, 1911

17

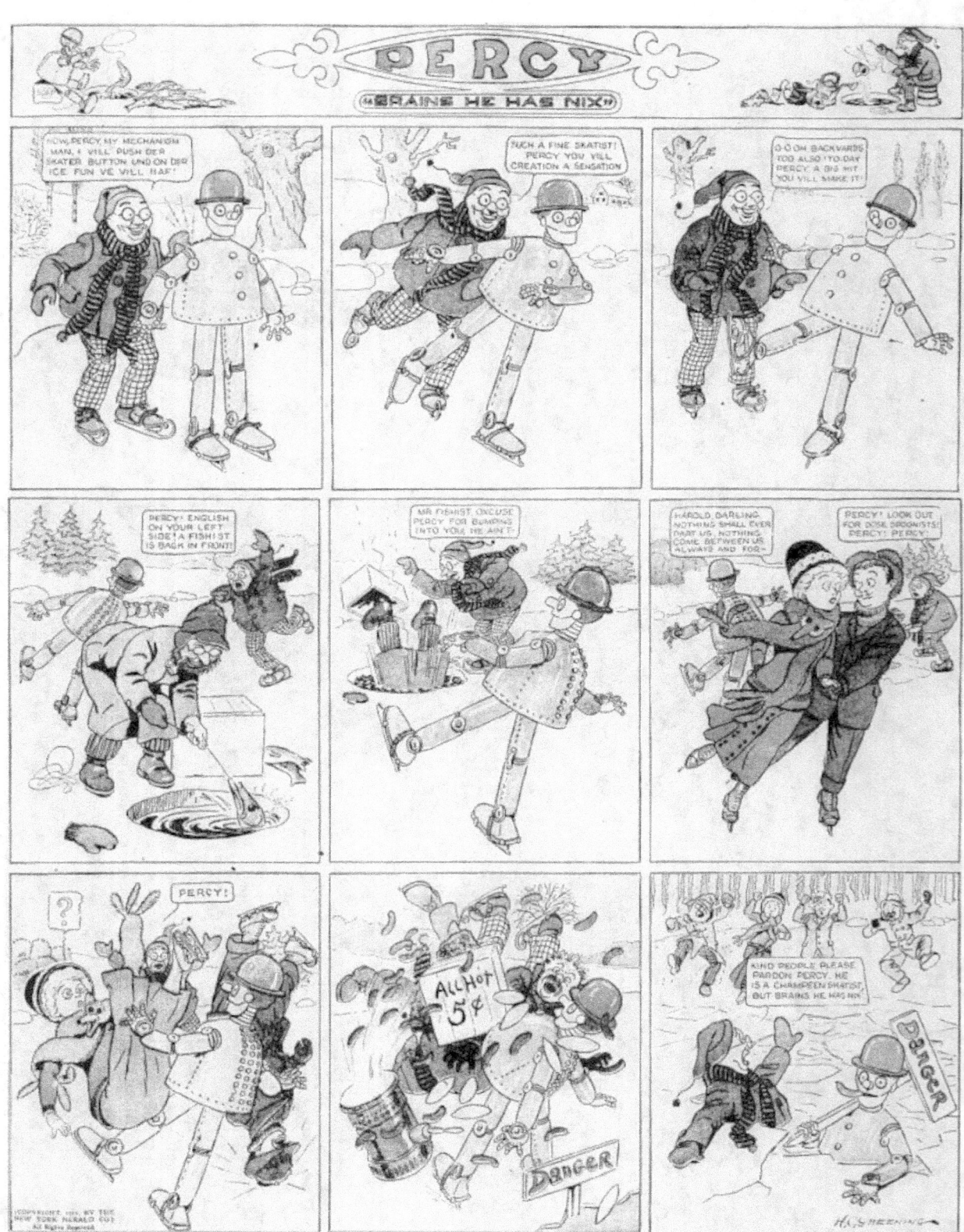

Percy: Brains He Has Nix by Harry Cornell Greening / Comic Strip #11 / Published in the Washington Evening Star December 10, 1911

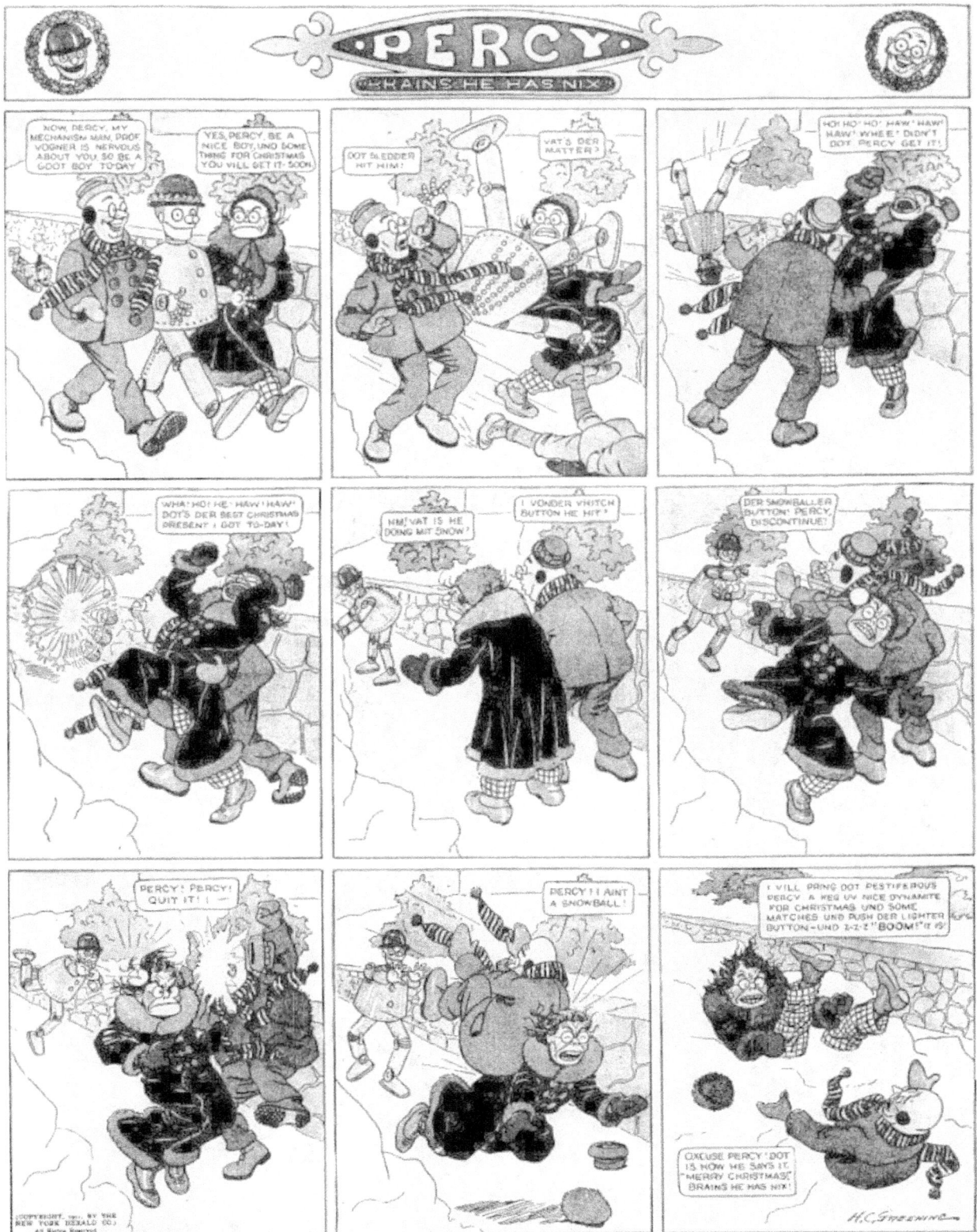

Percy: Brains He Has Nix by Harry Cornell Greening / Comic Strip #12 / Published in the Washington Evening Star December 17, 1911

19

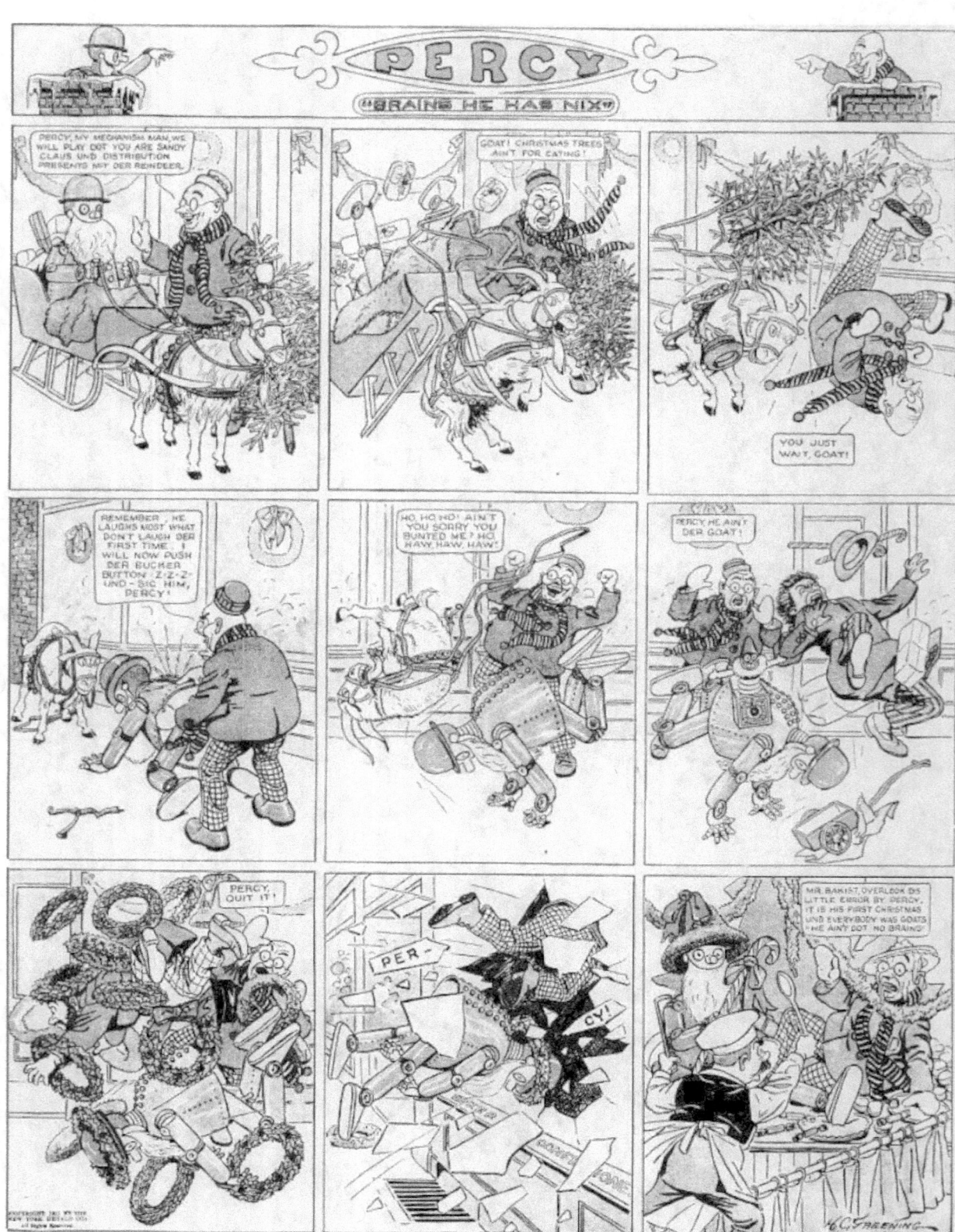

Percy: Brains He Has Nix by Harry Cornell Greening / Comic Strip #13 / Published in the Washington Evening Star December 24, 1911

20

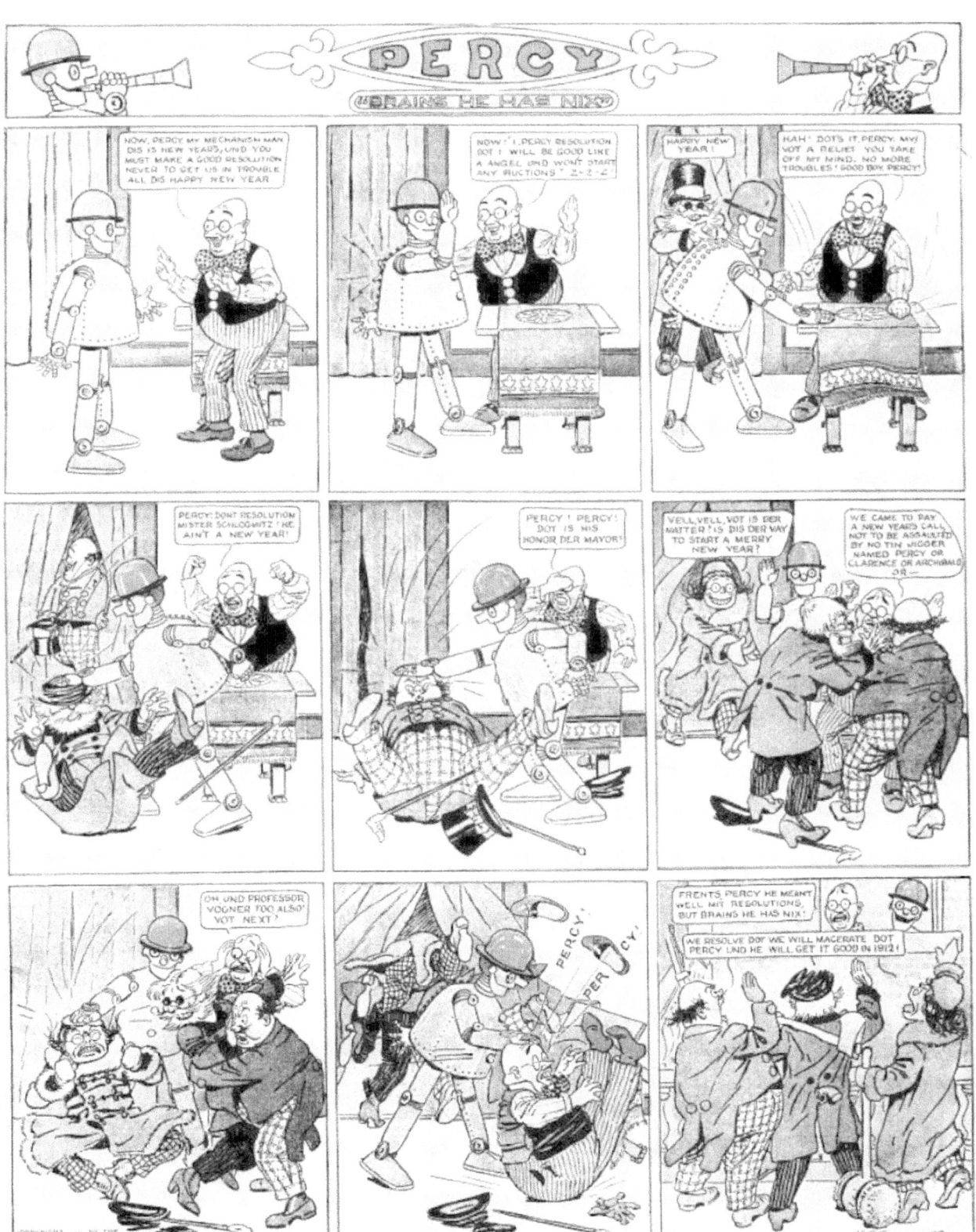

Percy: Brains He Has Nix by Harry Cornell Greening / Comic Strip #14 / Published in the Washington Evening Star December 31, 1911

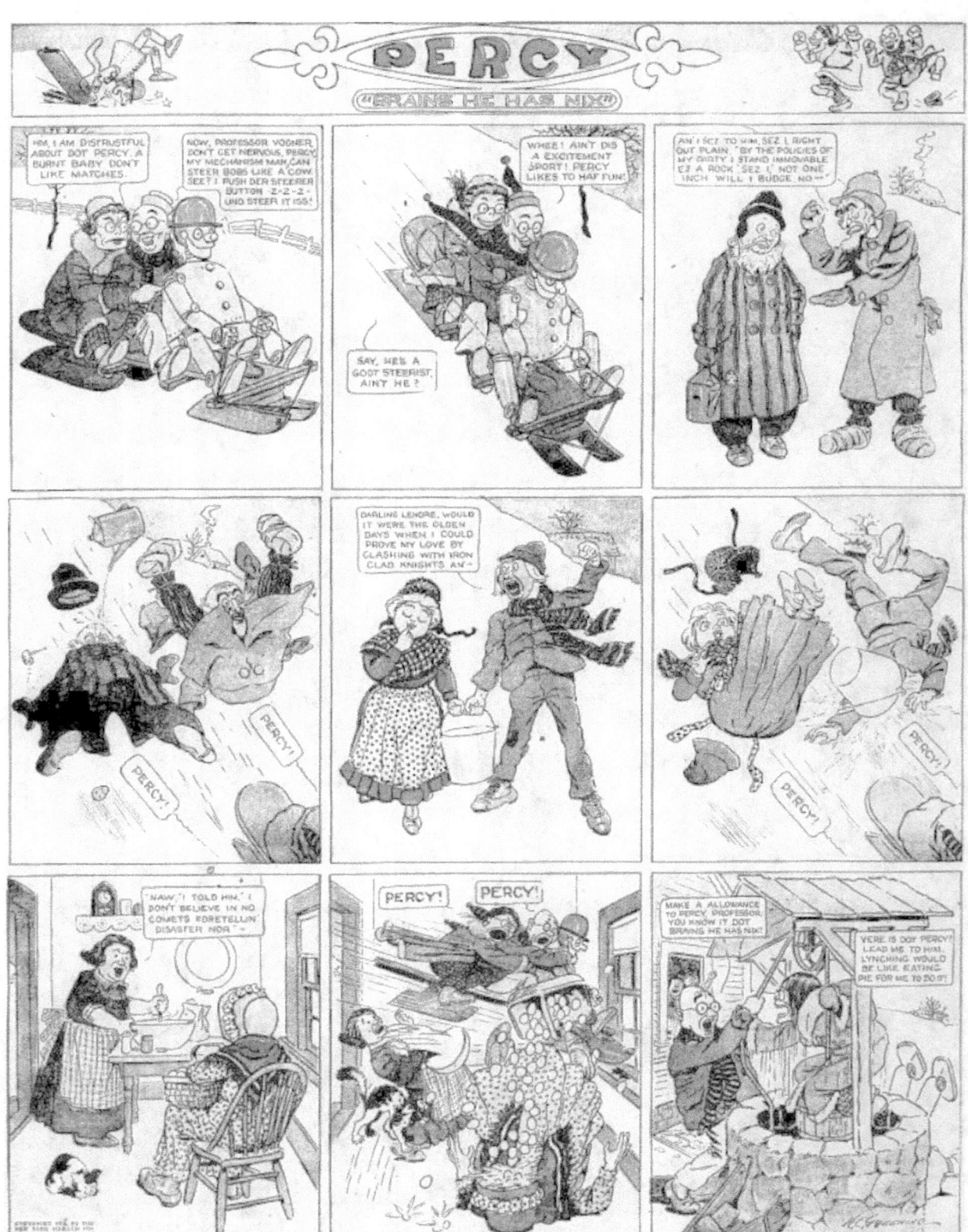

Percy: Brains He Has Nix by Harry Cornell Greening / Comic Strip #15 / Published in the Washington Evening Star January 7, 1912

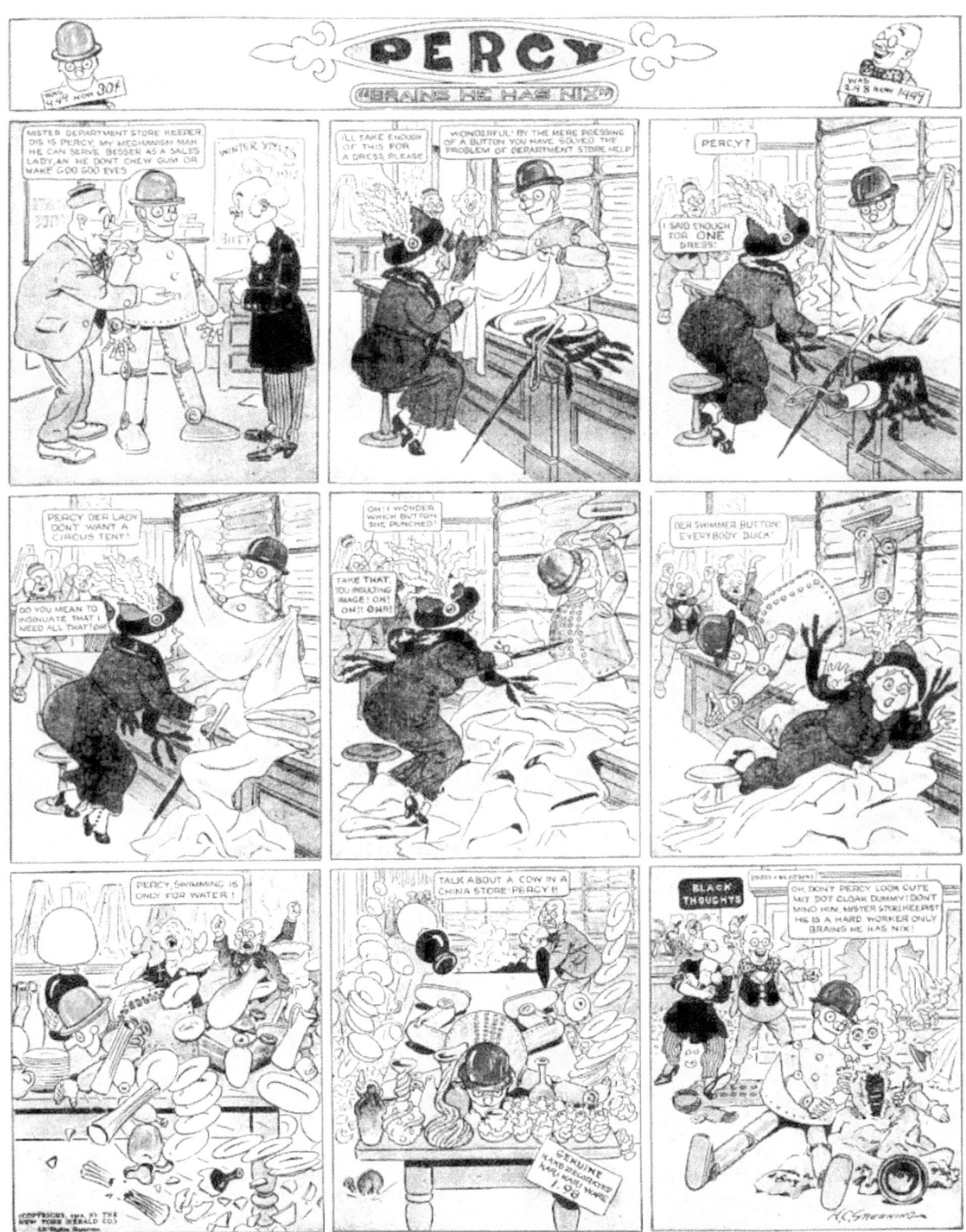

Percy: Brains He Has Nix by Harry Cornell Greening / Comic Strip #16 / Published in the Washington Evening Star January 14, 1912

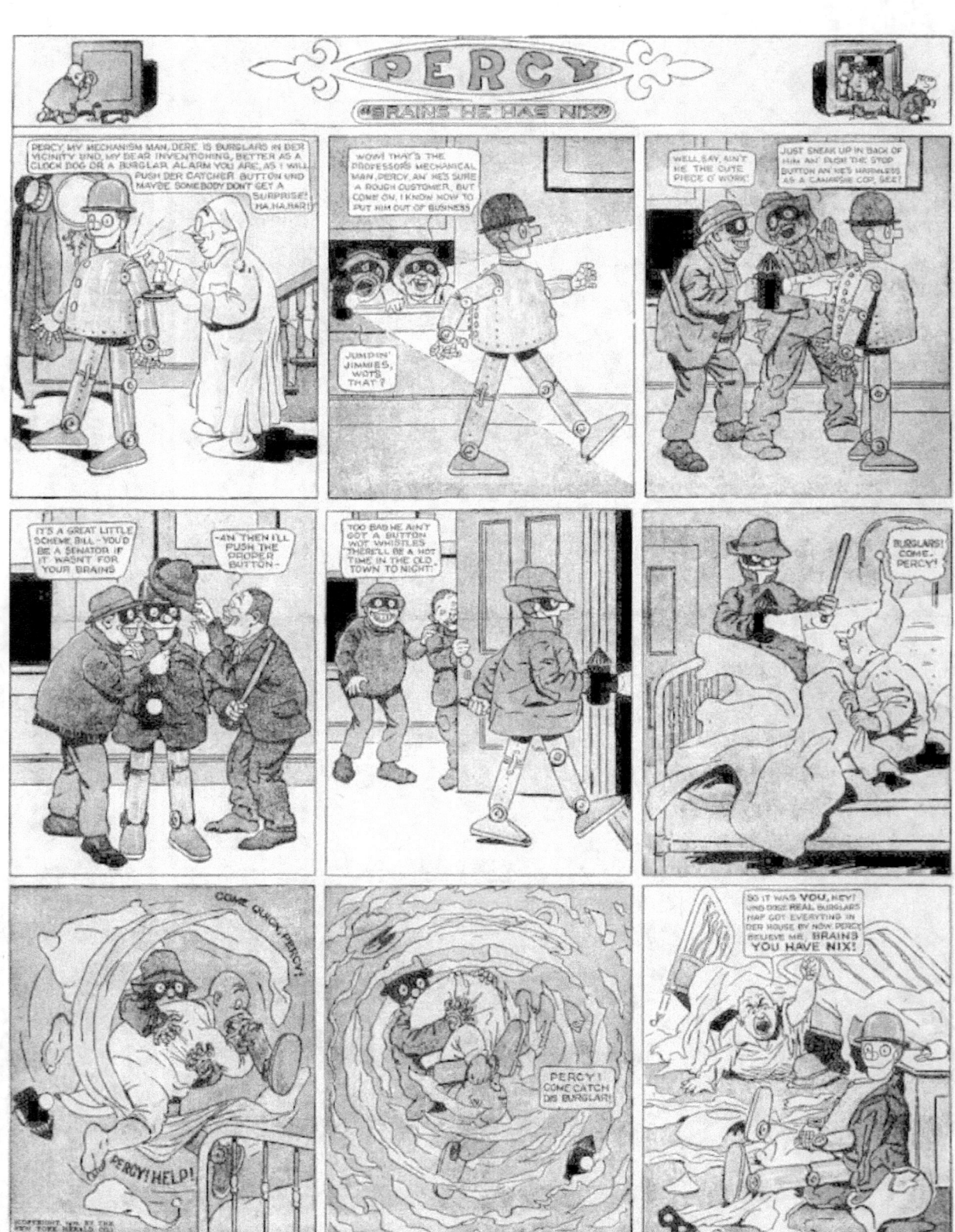

Percy: Brains He Has Nix by Harry Cornell Greening / Comic Strip #17 / Published in the Washington Evening Star January 21, 1912

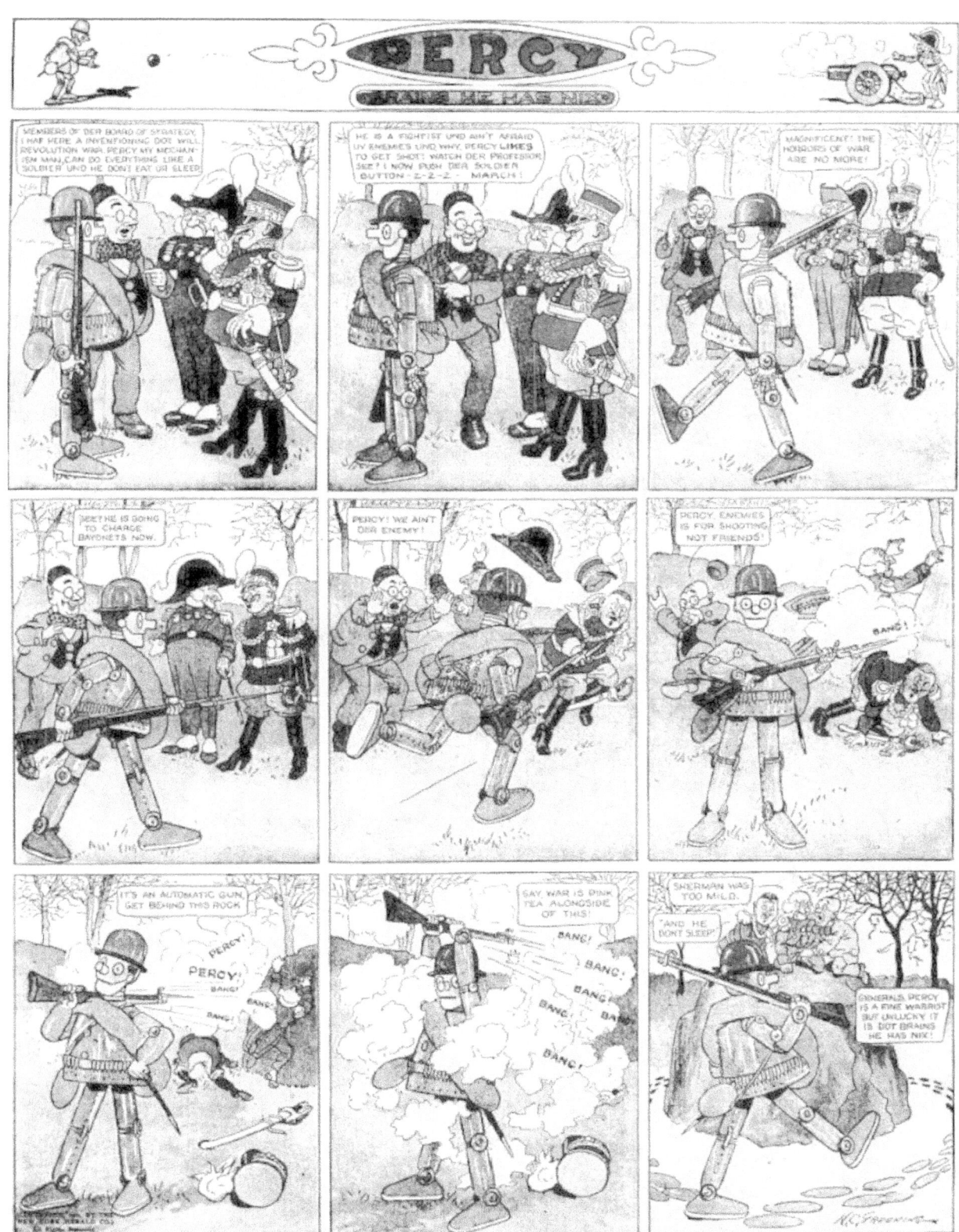

Percy: Brains He Has Nix by Harry Cornell Greening / Comic Strip #18 / Published in the Washington Evening Star January 28, 1912

25

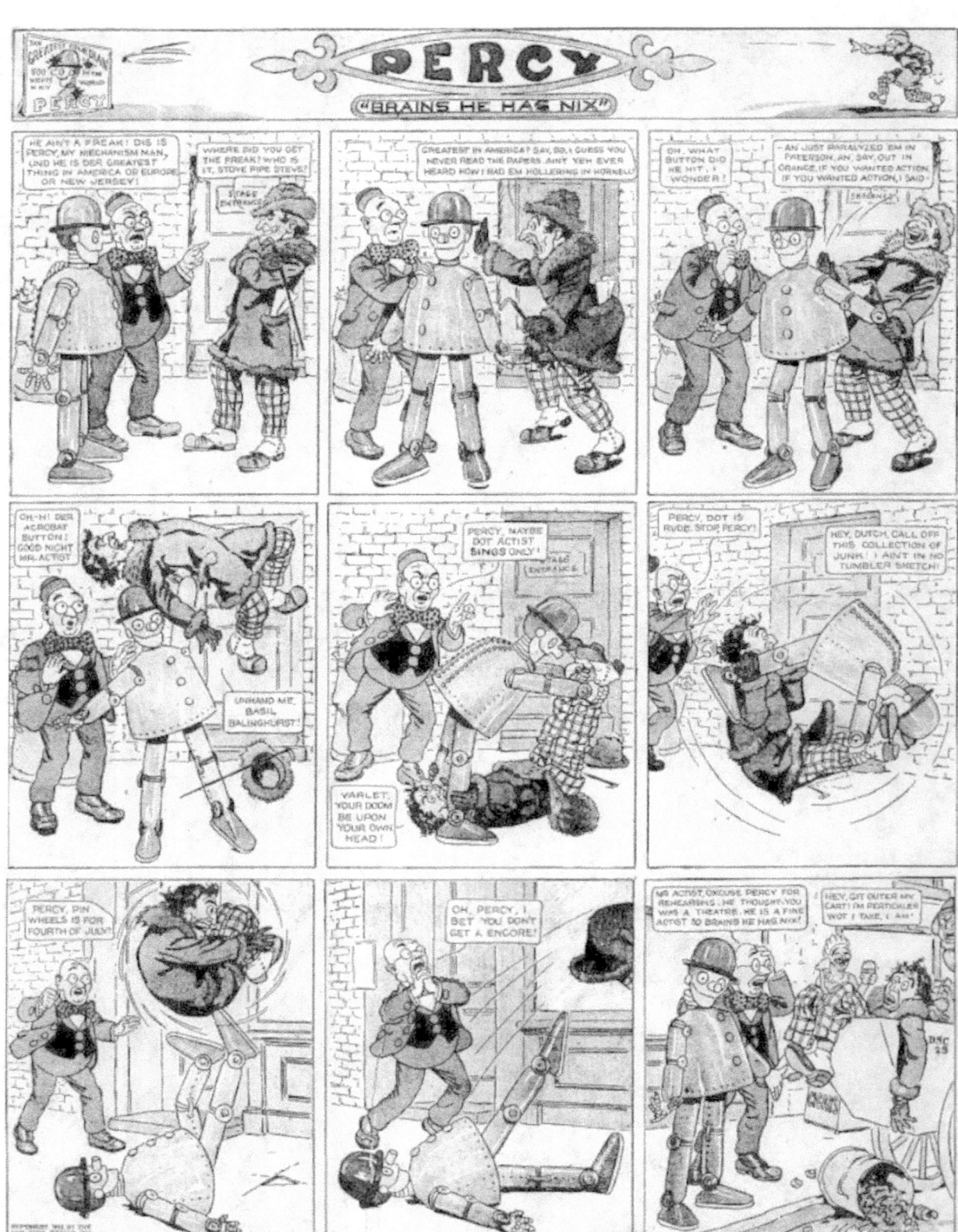

Percy: Brains He Has Nix by Harry Cornell Greening / Comic Strip #19 / Published in the Washington Evening Star February 4, 1912

26

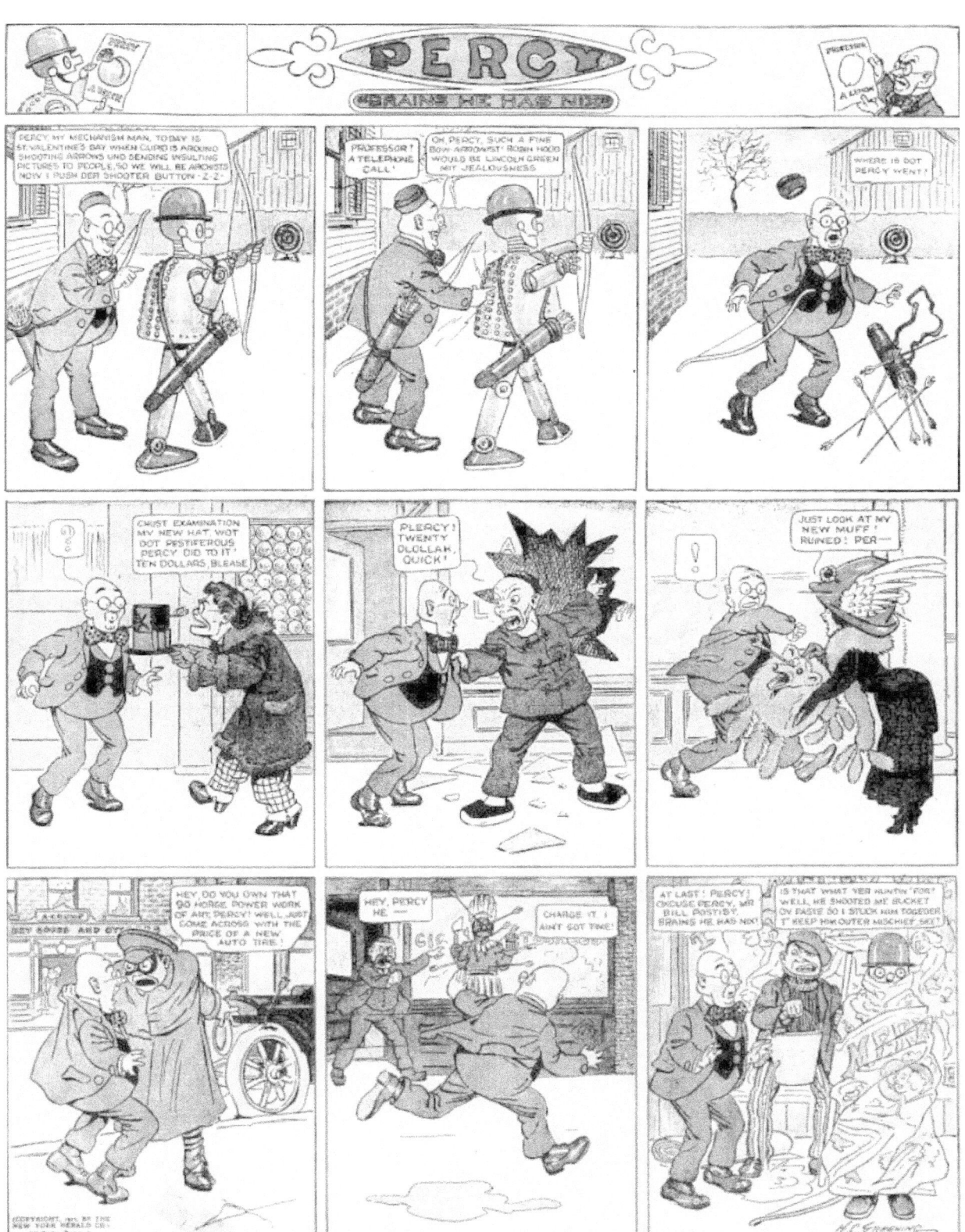

Percy: Brains He Has Nix by Harry Cornell Greening / Comic Strip #20 / Published in the Washington Evening Star February 11, 1912

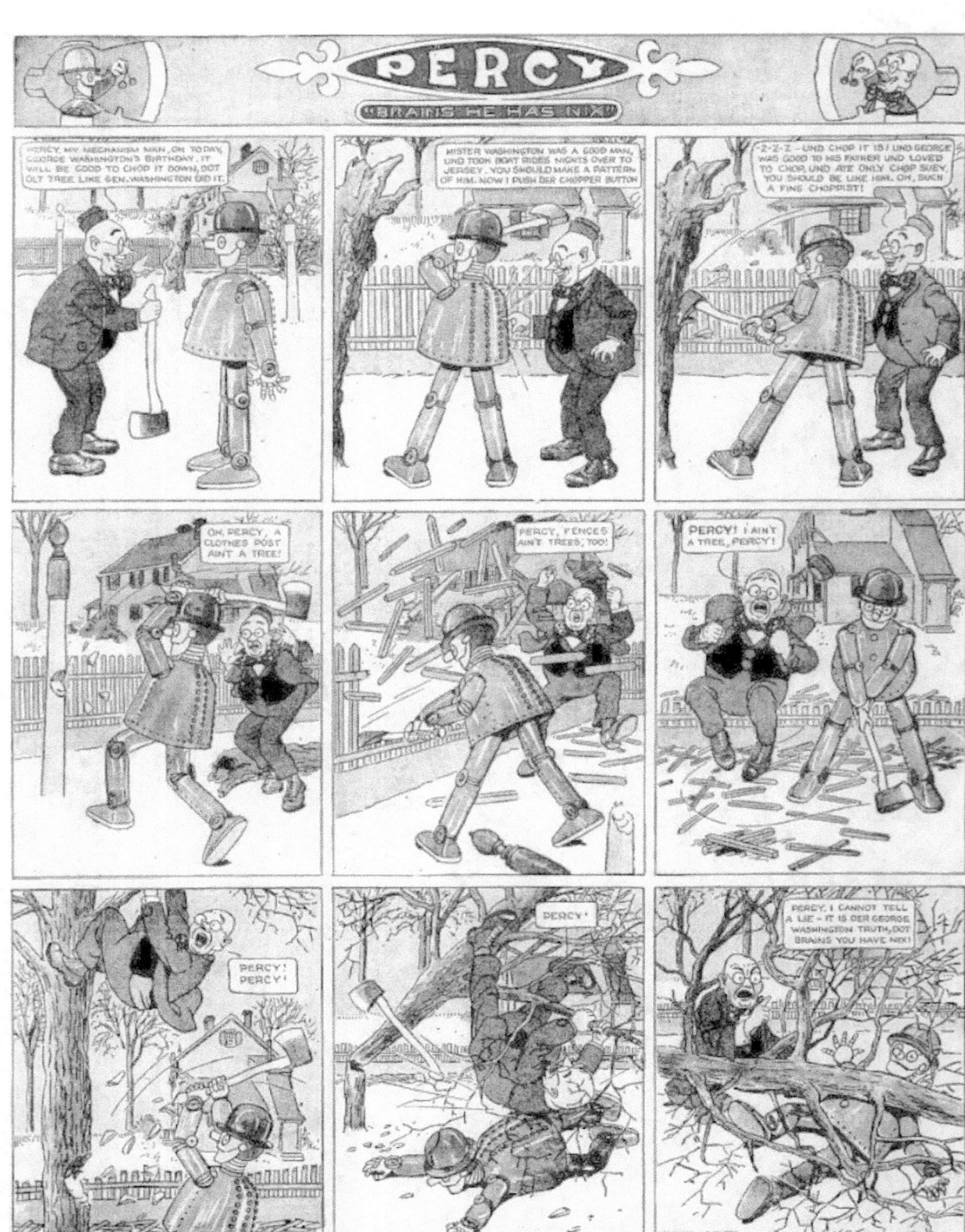

Percy: Brains He Has Nix by Harry Cornell Greening / Comic Strip #21 / Published in the Washington Evening Star February 18, 1912

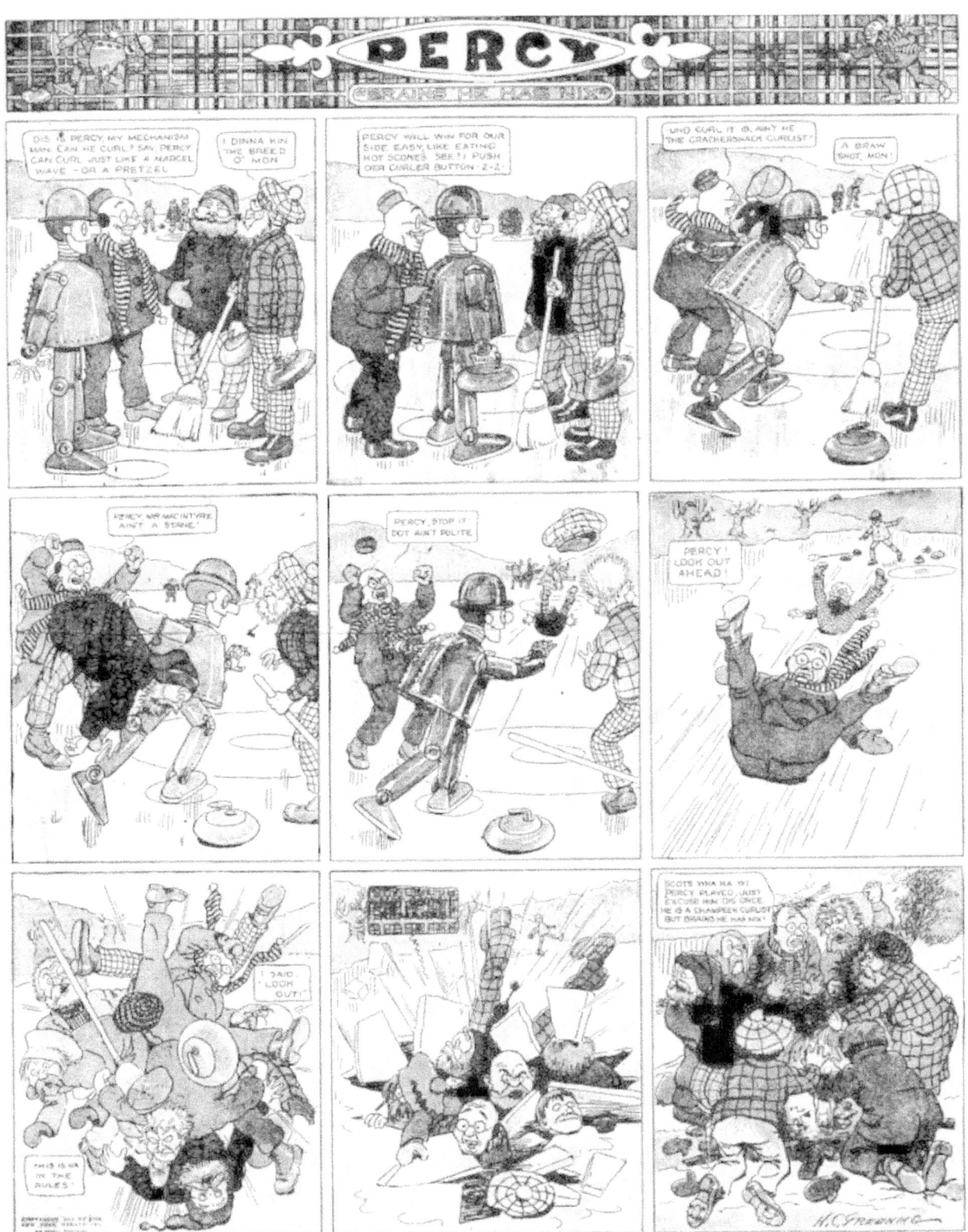

Percy: Brains He Has Nix by Harry Cornell Greening / Comic Strip #22 / Published in the Washington Evening Star February 25, 1912

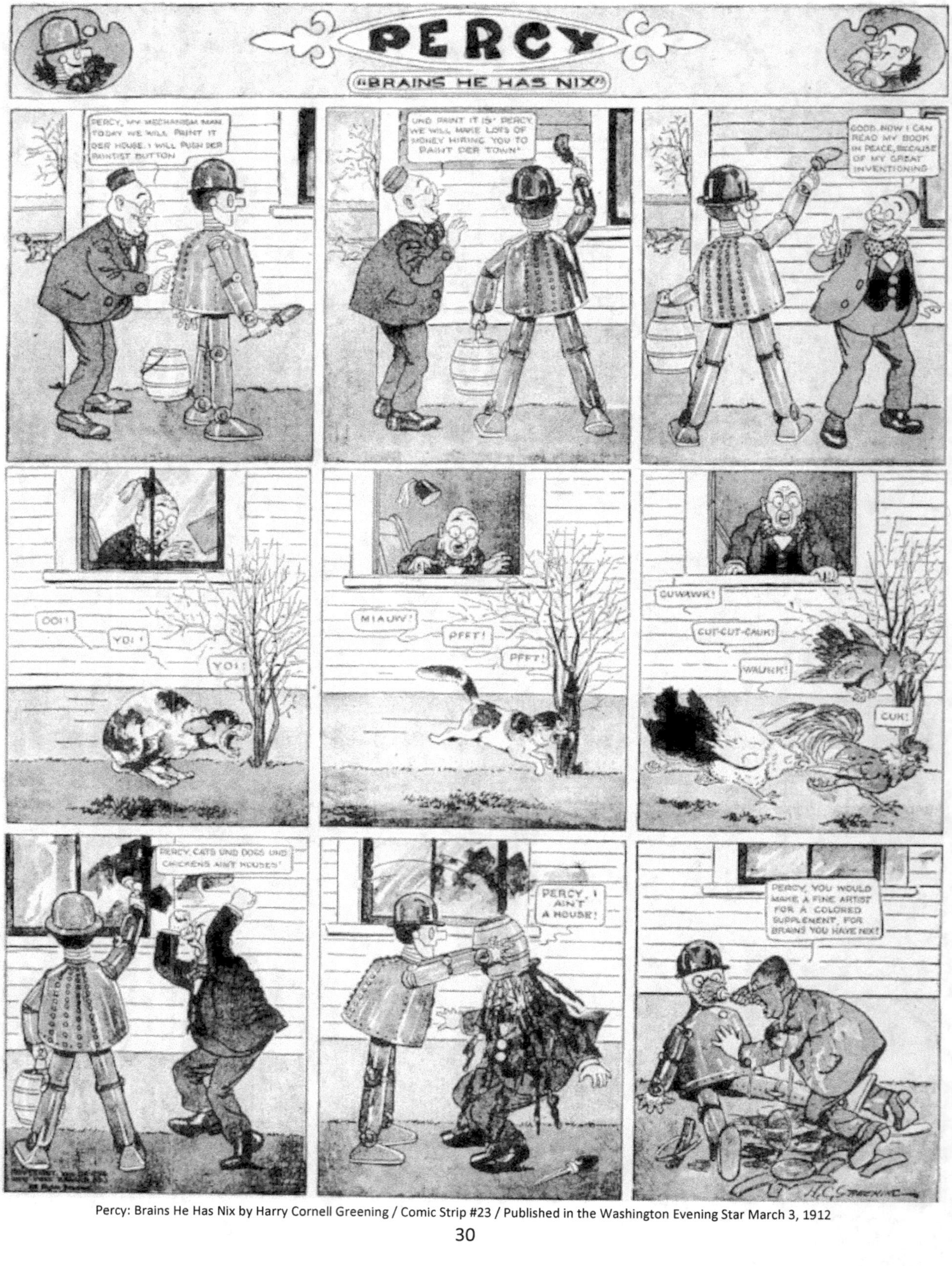

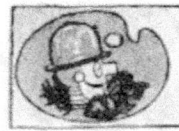 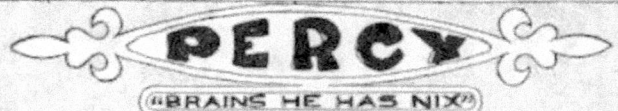 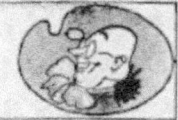

Percy: Brains He Has Nix by Harry Cornell Greening / Comic Strip #23 / Published in the Washington Evening Star March 3, 1912

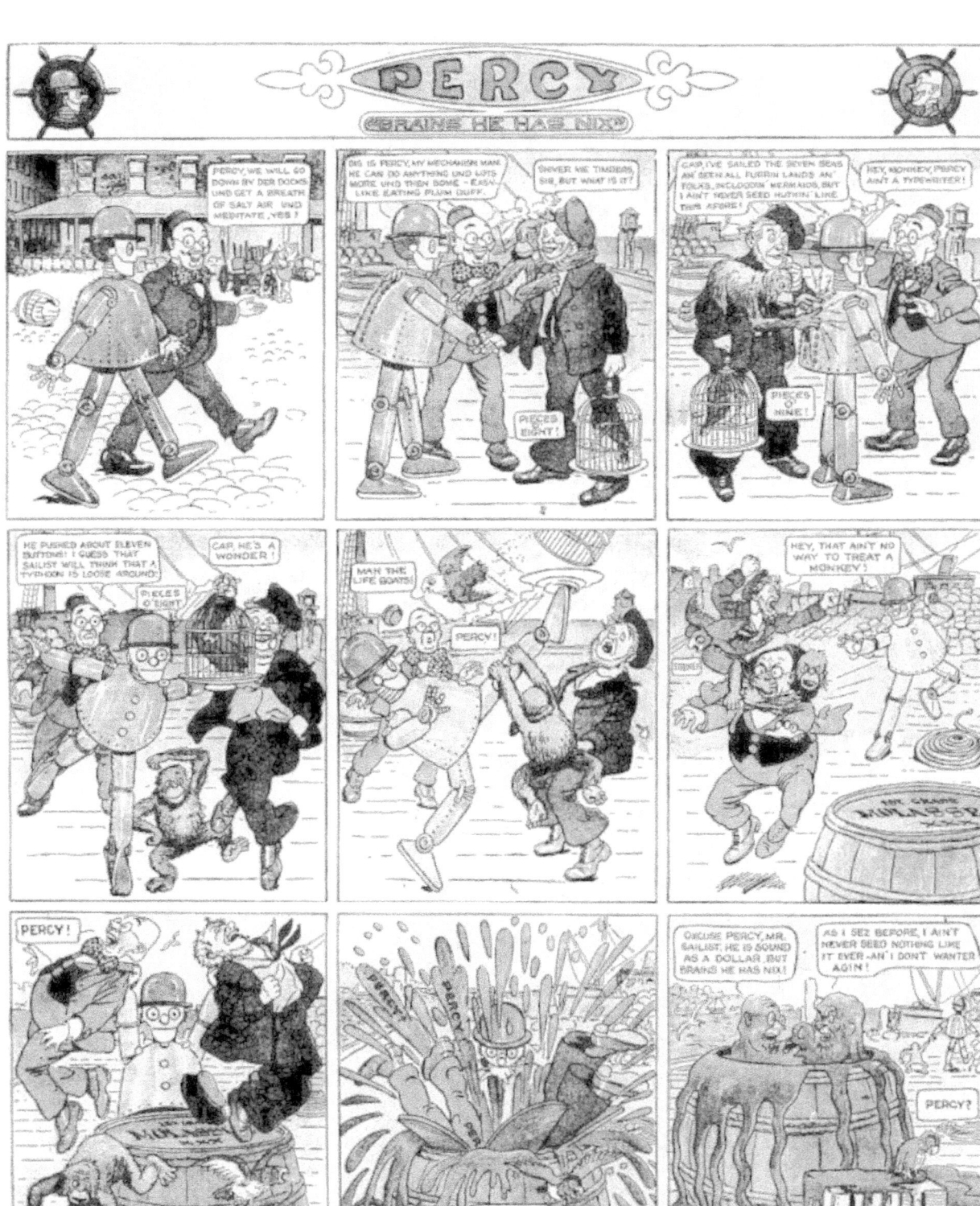

Percy: Brains He Has Nix by Harry Cornell Greening / Comic Strip #24 / Published in the Washington Evening Star March 10, 1912

31

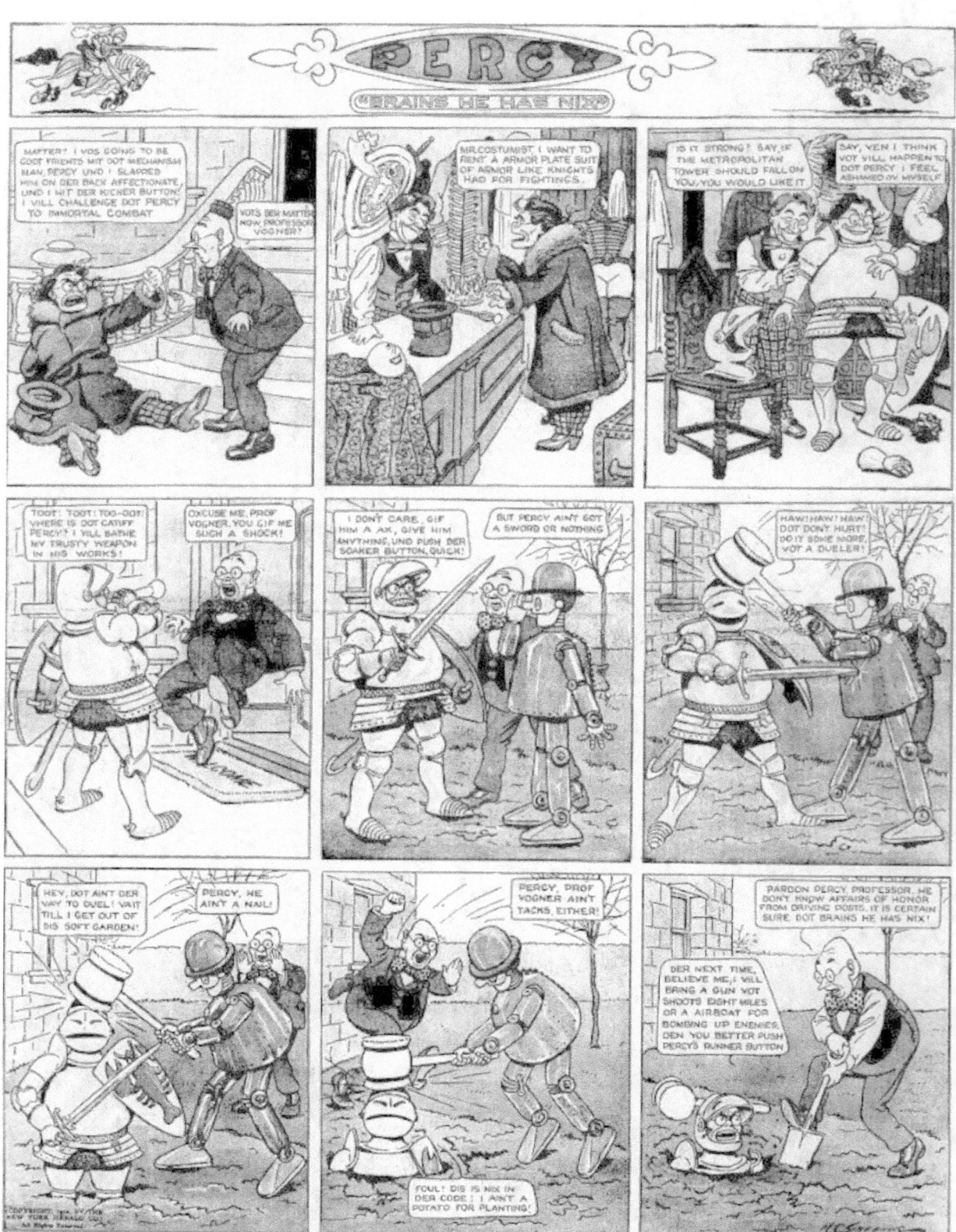

Percy: Brains He Has Nix by Harry Cornell Greening / Comic Strip #25 / Published in the Washington Evening Star March 17, 1912

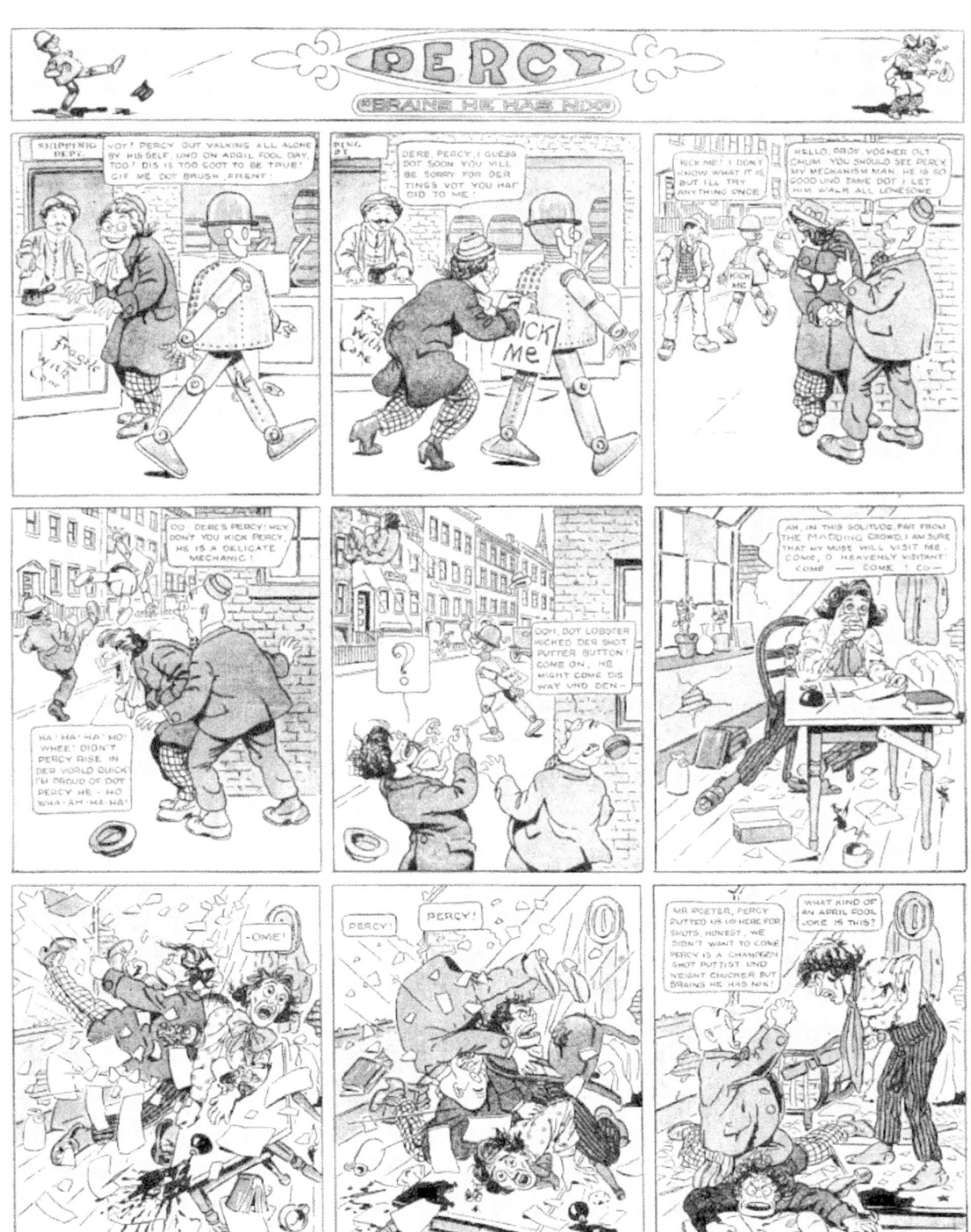

Percy: Brains He Has Nix by Harry Cornell Greening / Comic Strip #26 / Published in the Washington Evening Star March 24, 1912

33

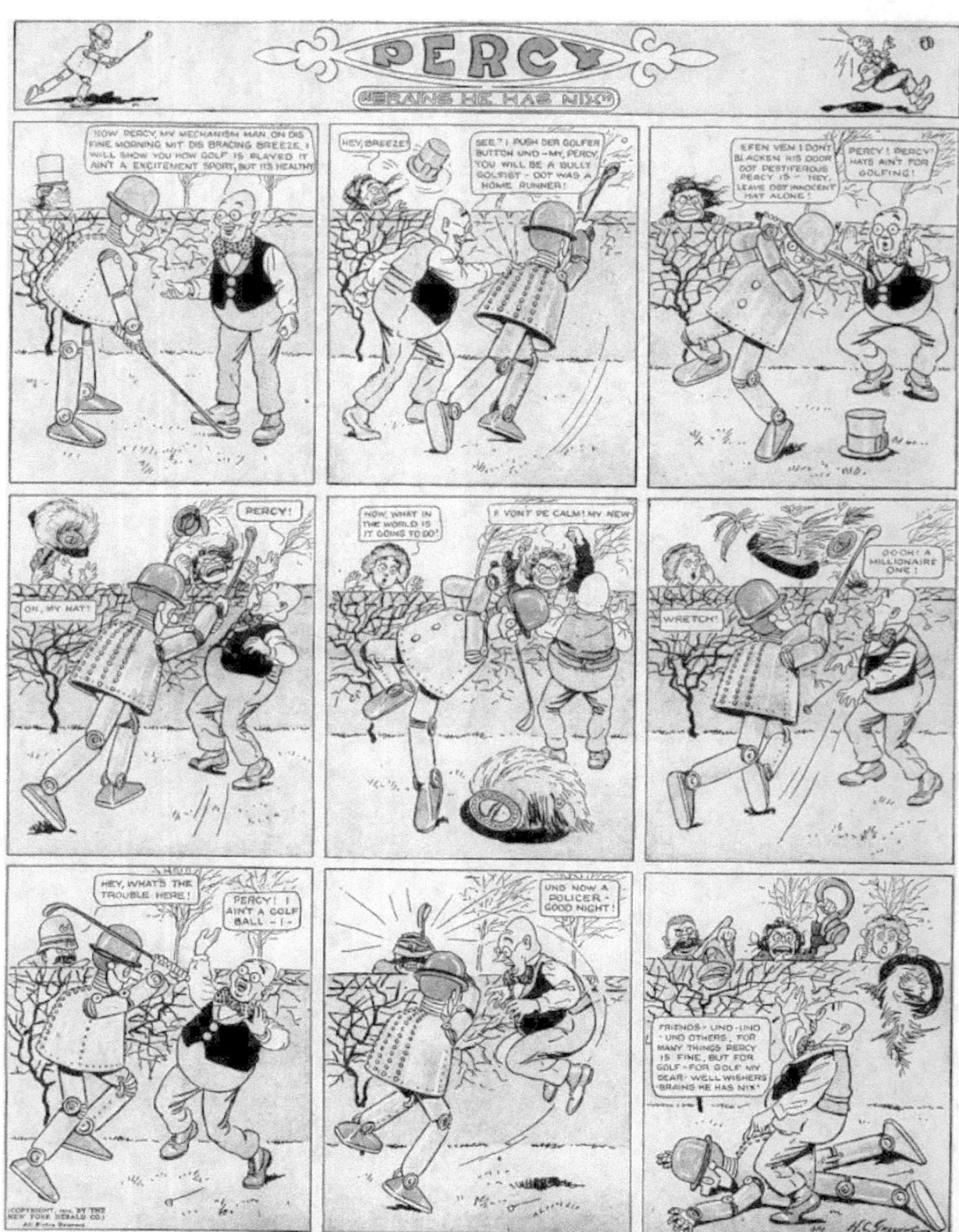

Percy: Brains He Has Nix by Harry Cornell Greening / Comic Strip #27 / Published in the Washington Evening Star March 31, 1912

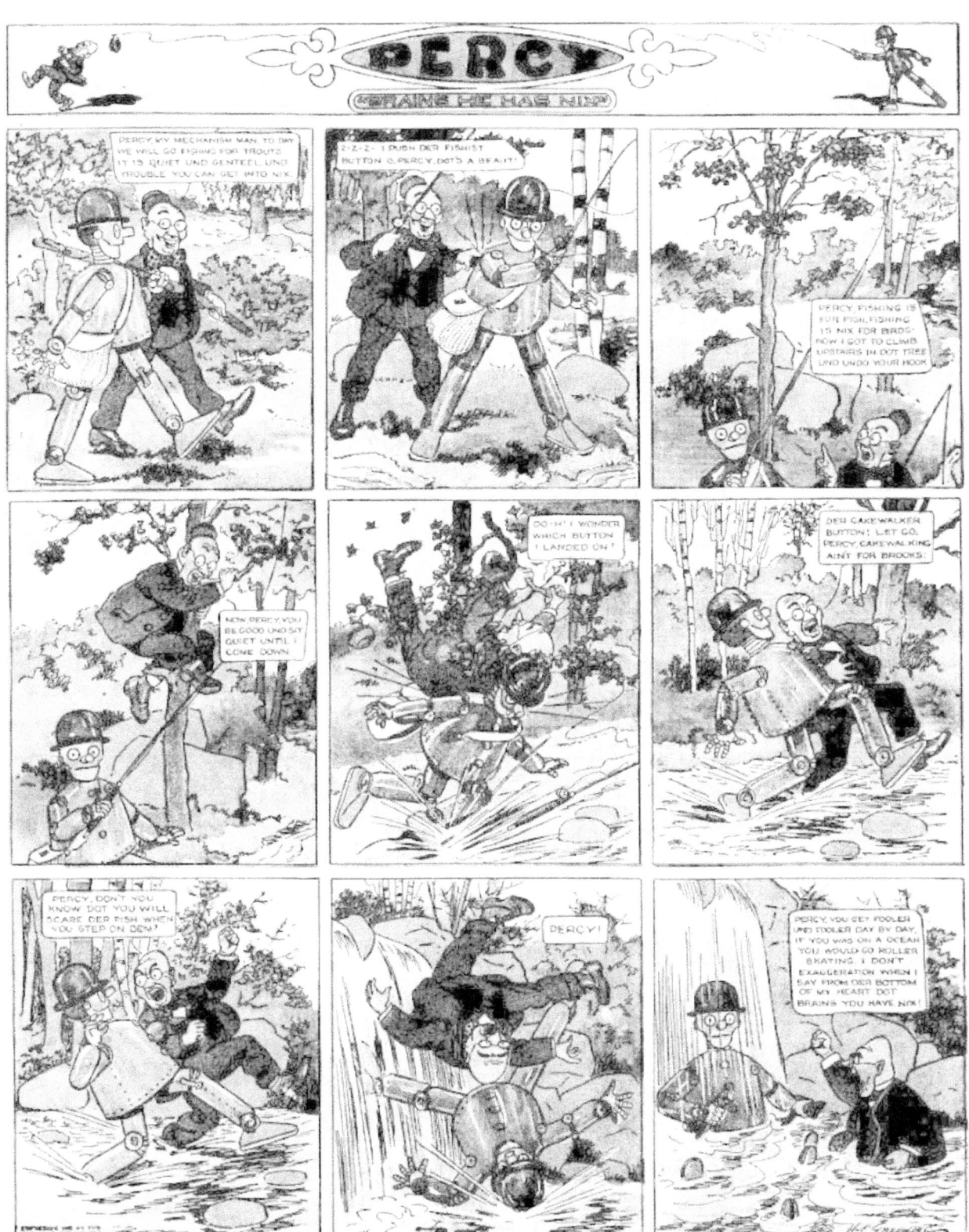

Percy: Brains He Has Nix by Harry Cornell Greening / Comic Strip #28 / Published in the Washington Evening Star April 7, 1912

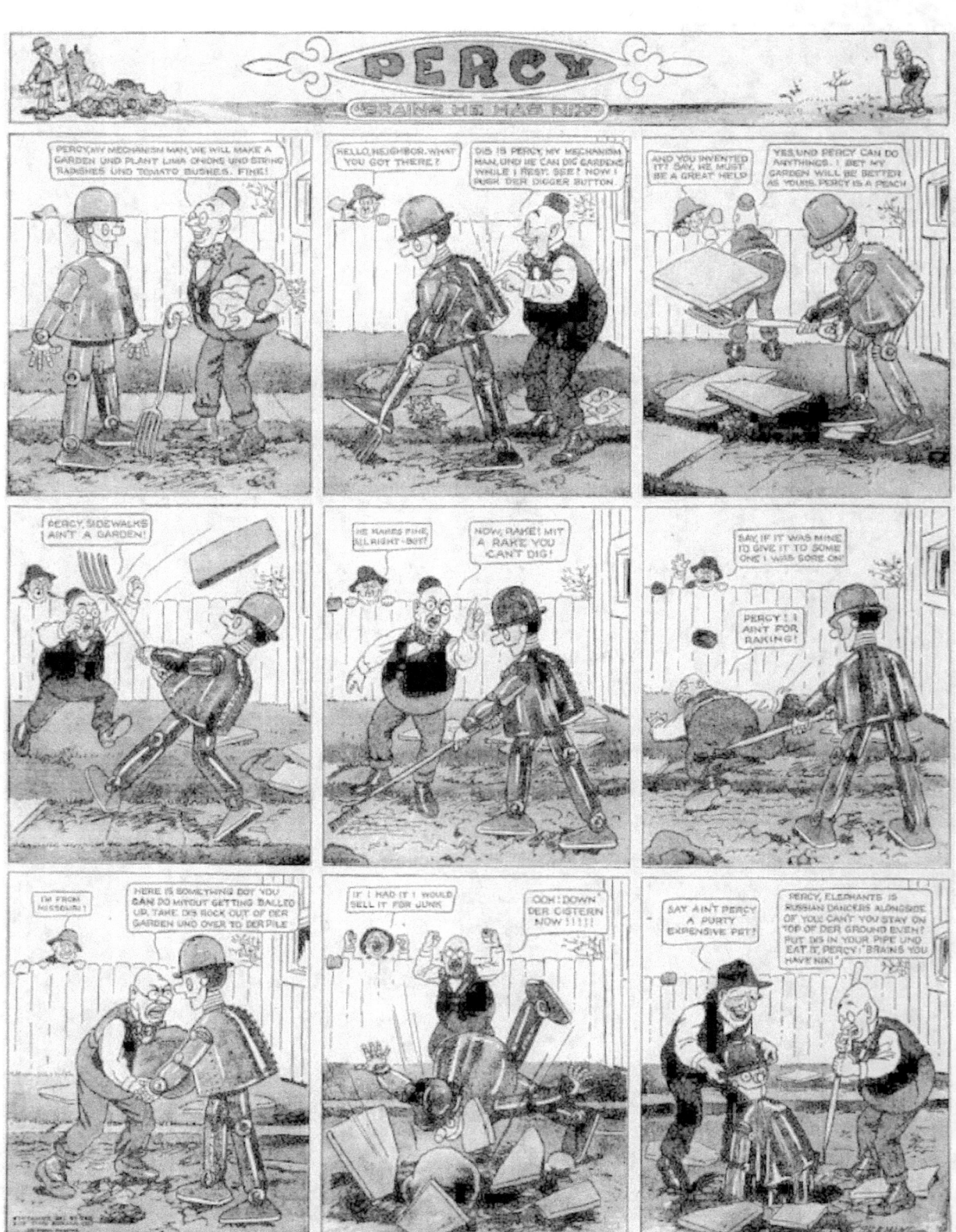

Percy: Brains He Has Nix by Harry Cornell Greening / Comic Strip #29 / Published in the Washington Evening Star April 14, 1912

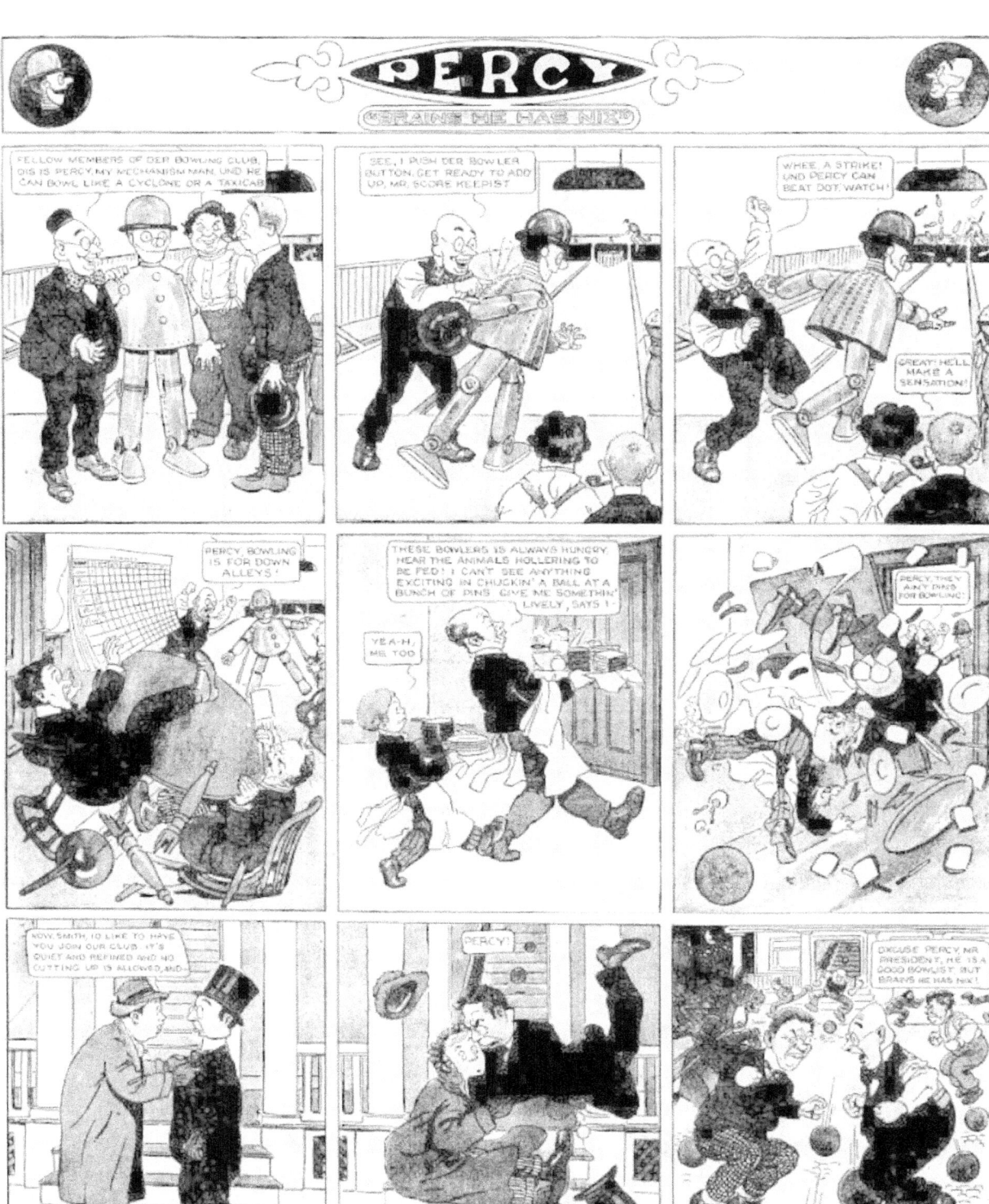

Percy: Brains He Has Nix by Harry Cornell Greening / Comic Strip #30 / Published in the Washington Evening Star April 21, 1912

37

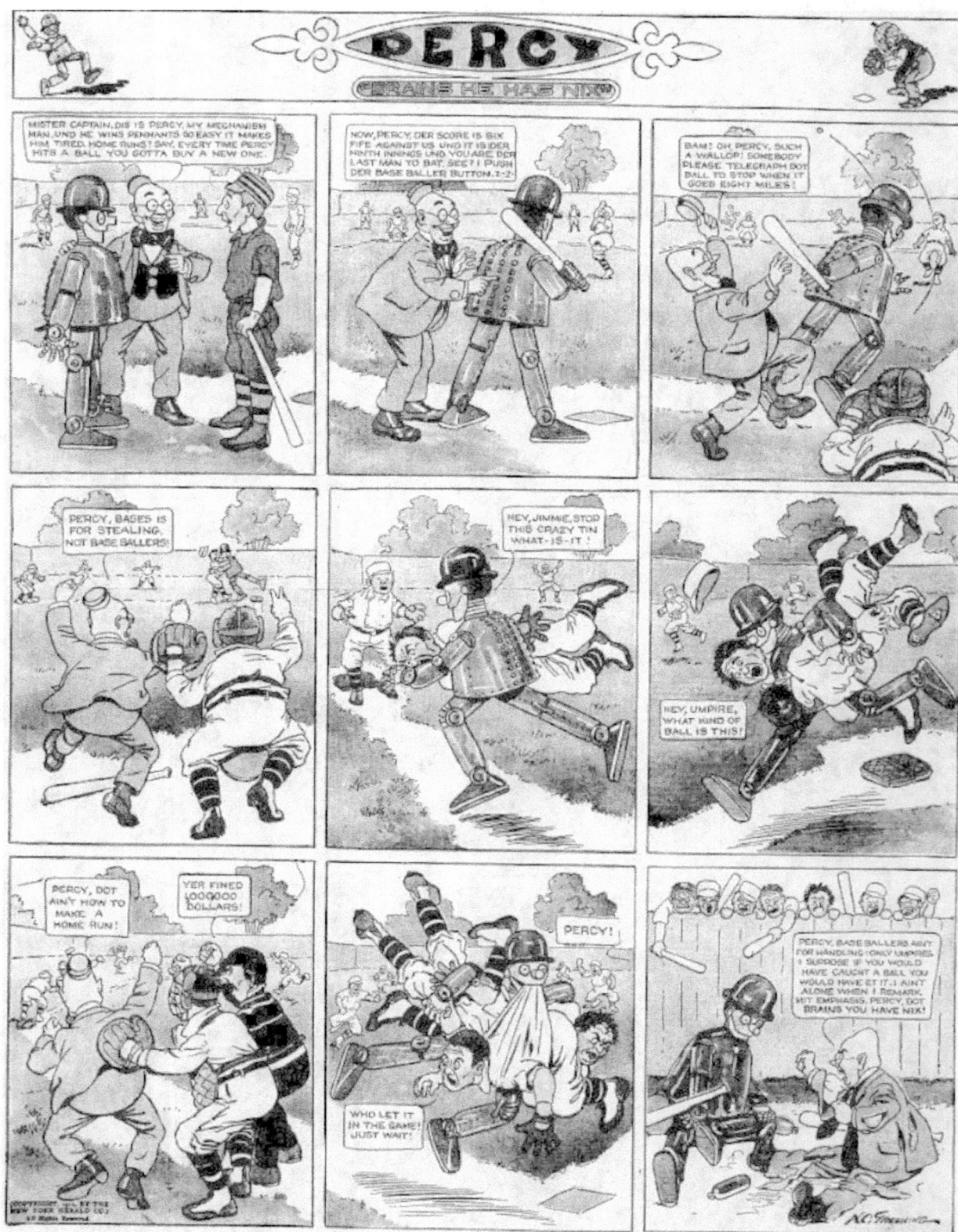

Percy: Brains He Has Nix by Harry Cornell Greening / Comic Strip #31 / Published in the Washington Evening Star April 28, 1912

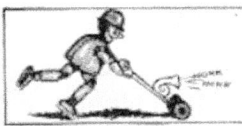
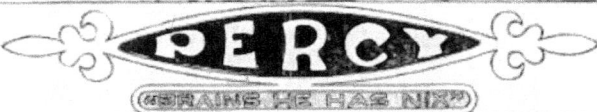
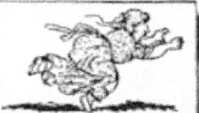
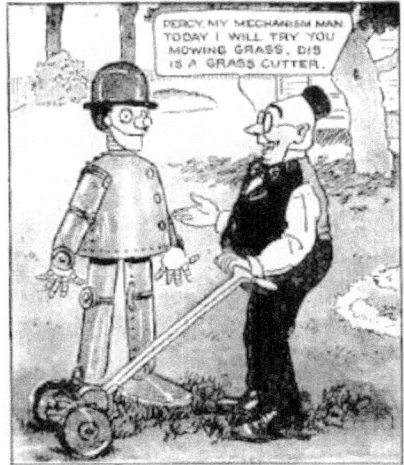
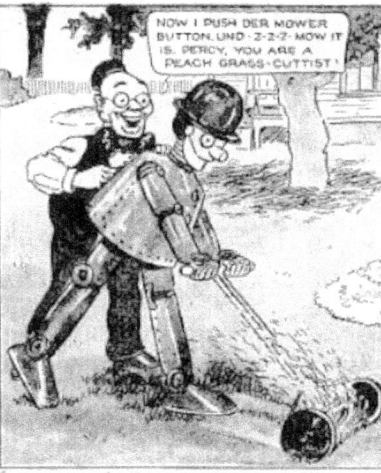
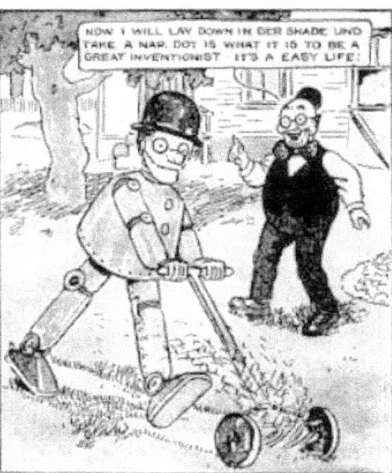
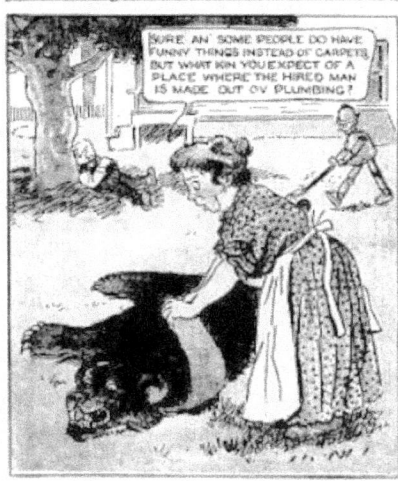
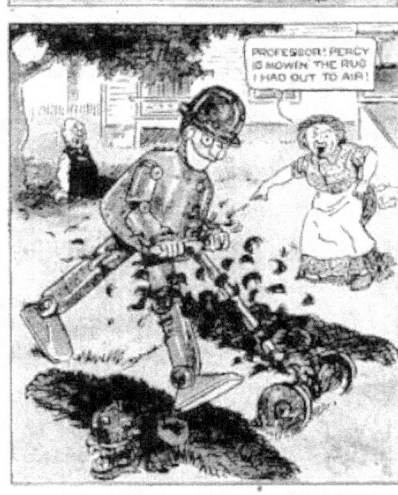
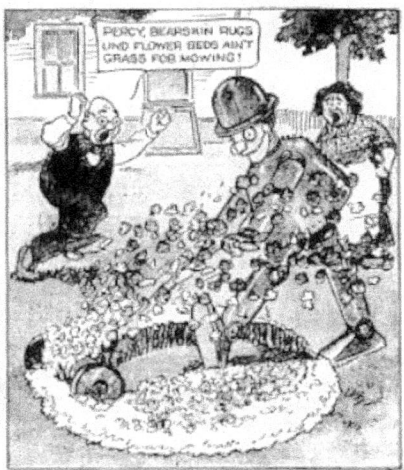
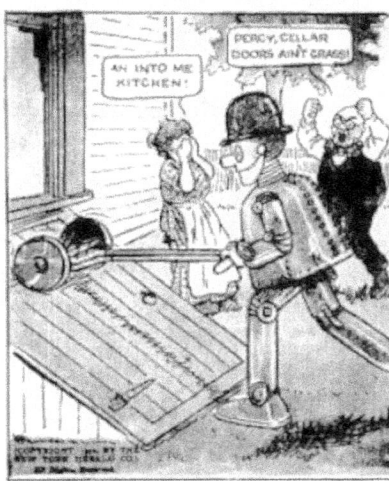
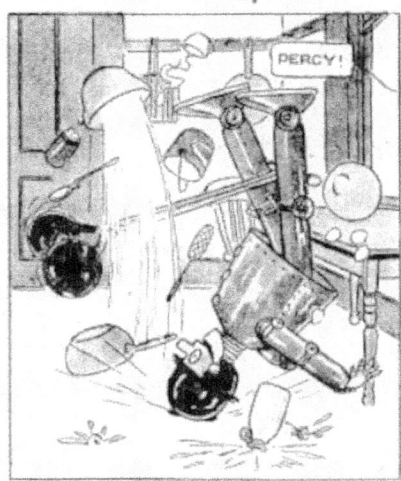
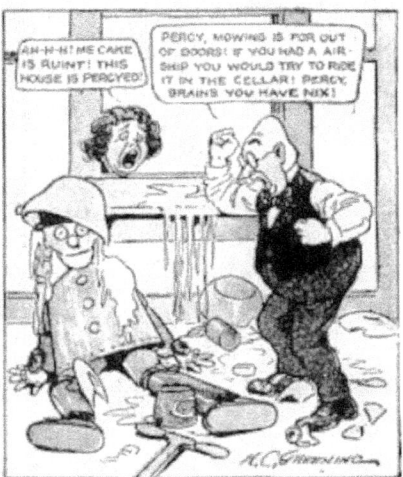

Percy: Brains He Has Nix by Harry Cornell Greening / Comic Strip #32 / Published in the Washington Evening Star May 5, 1912

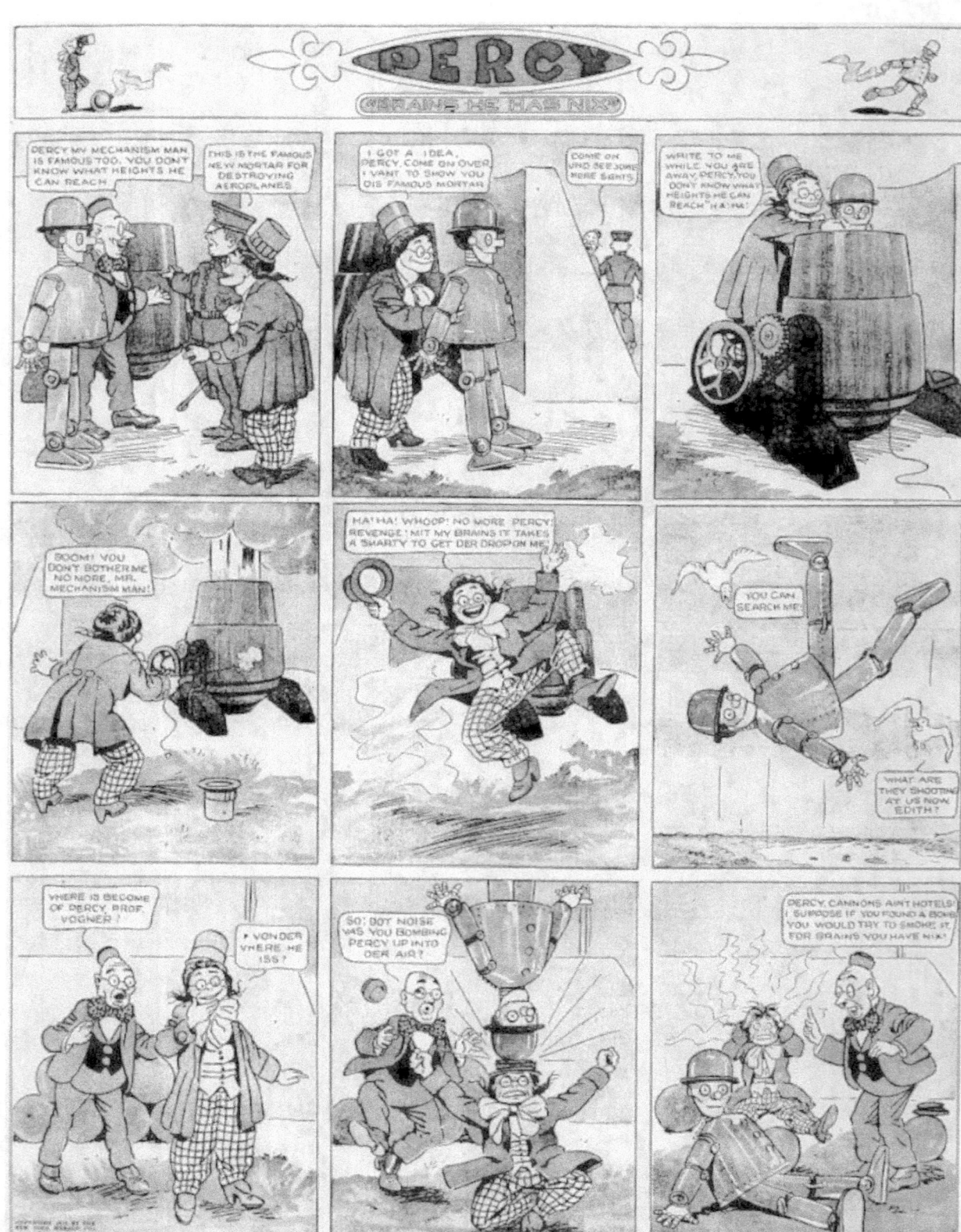

Percy: Brains He Has Nix by Harry Cornell Greening / Comic Strip #33 / Published in the Washington Evening Star May 12, 1912

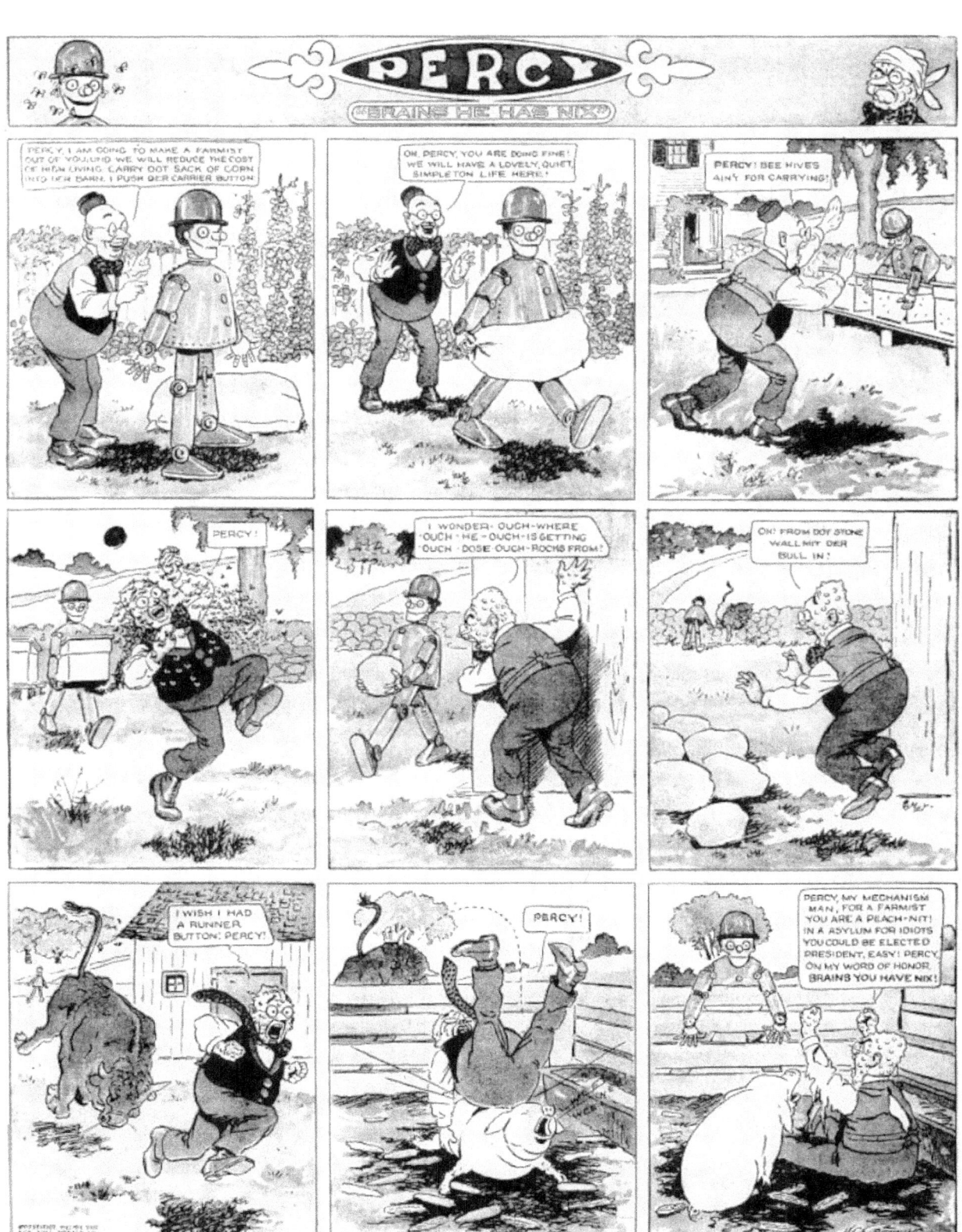

Percy: Brains He Has Nix by Harry Cornell Greening / Comic Strip #34 / Published in the Washington Evening Star May 19, 1912

41

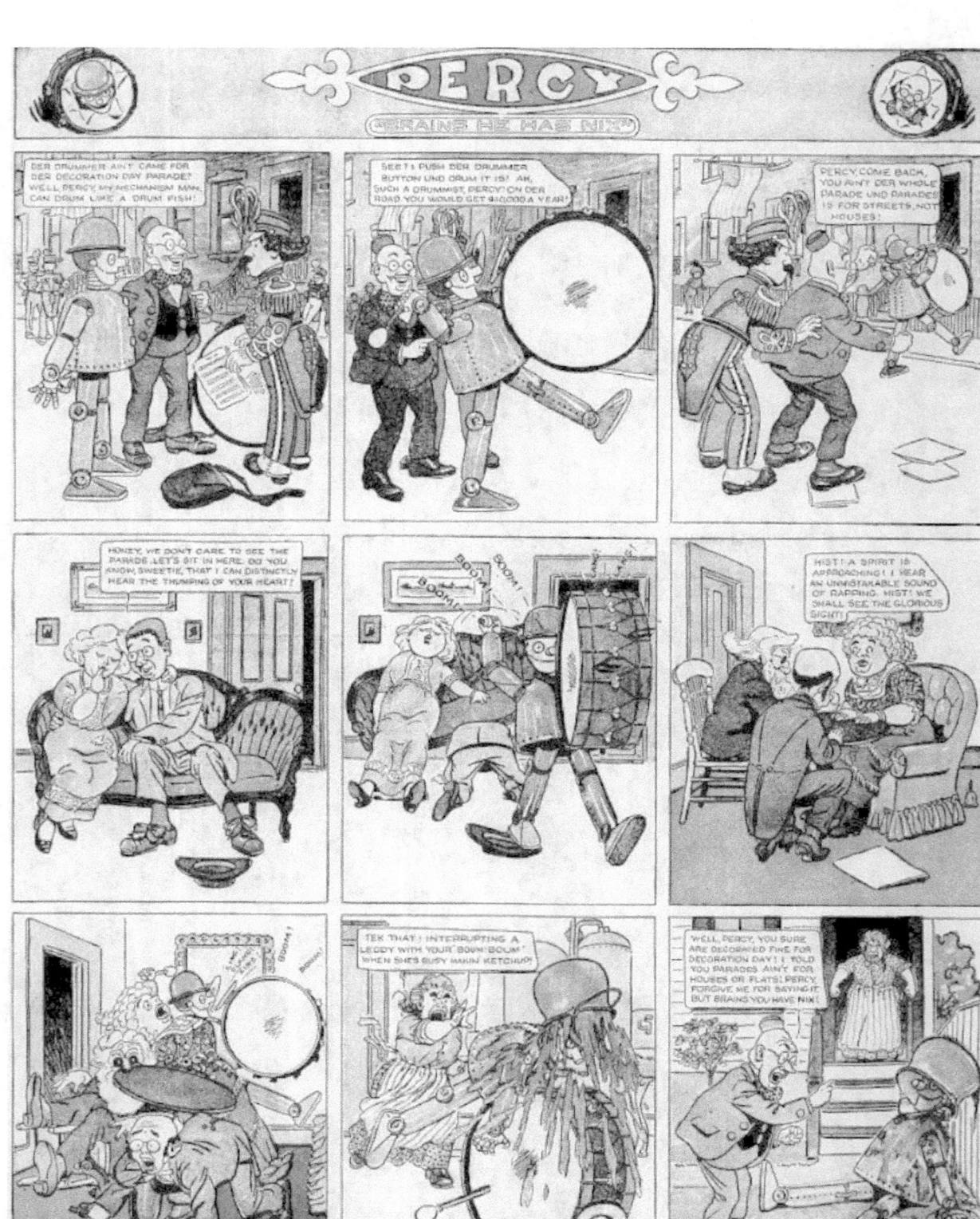

Percy: Brains He Has Nix by Harry Cornell Greening / Comic Strip #35 / Published in the Washington Evening Star May 26, 1912

42

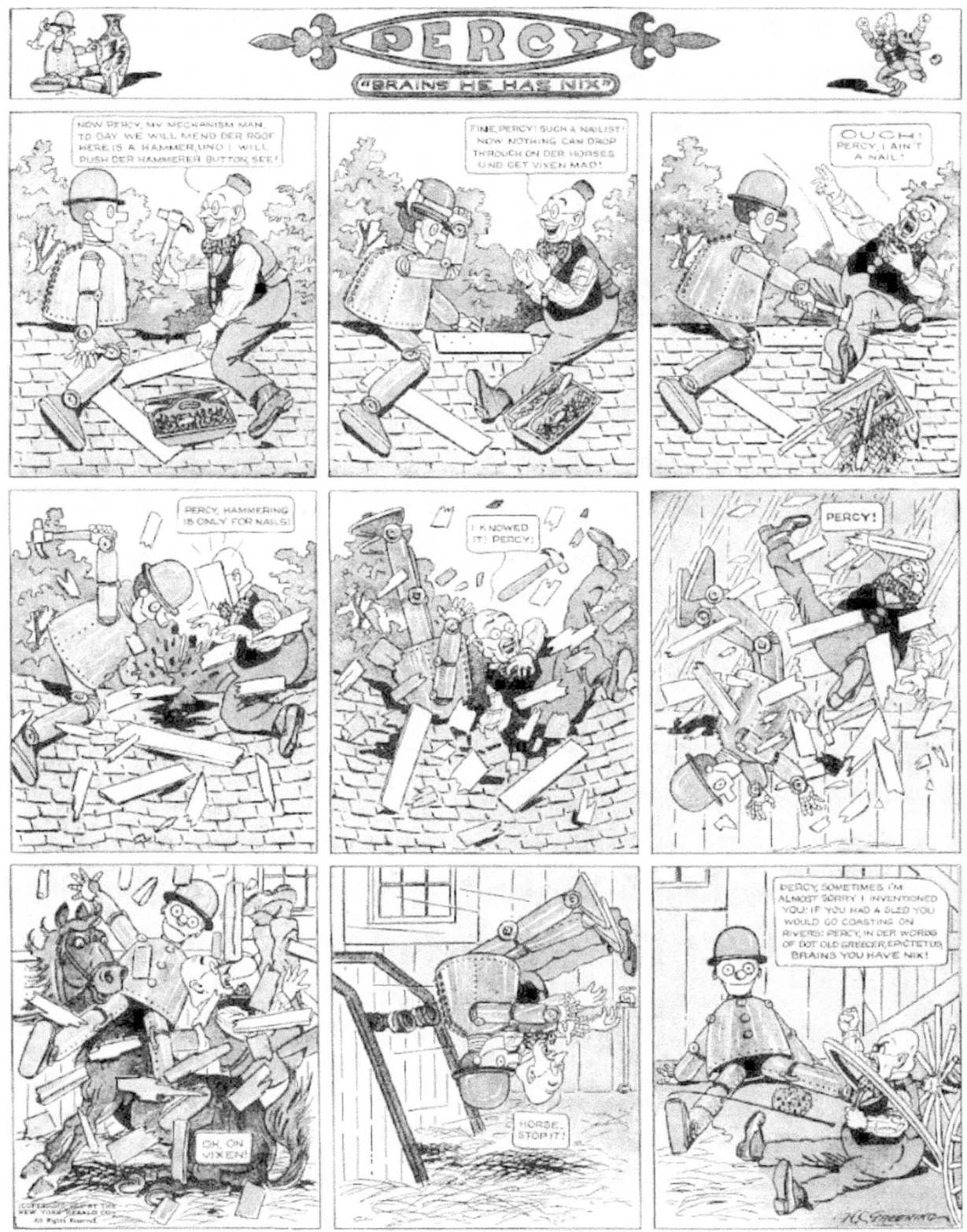

Percy: Brains He Has Nix by Harry Cornell Greening / Comic Strip #36 / Published in the Washington Evening Star June 2, 1912

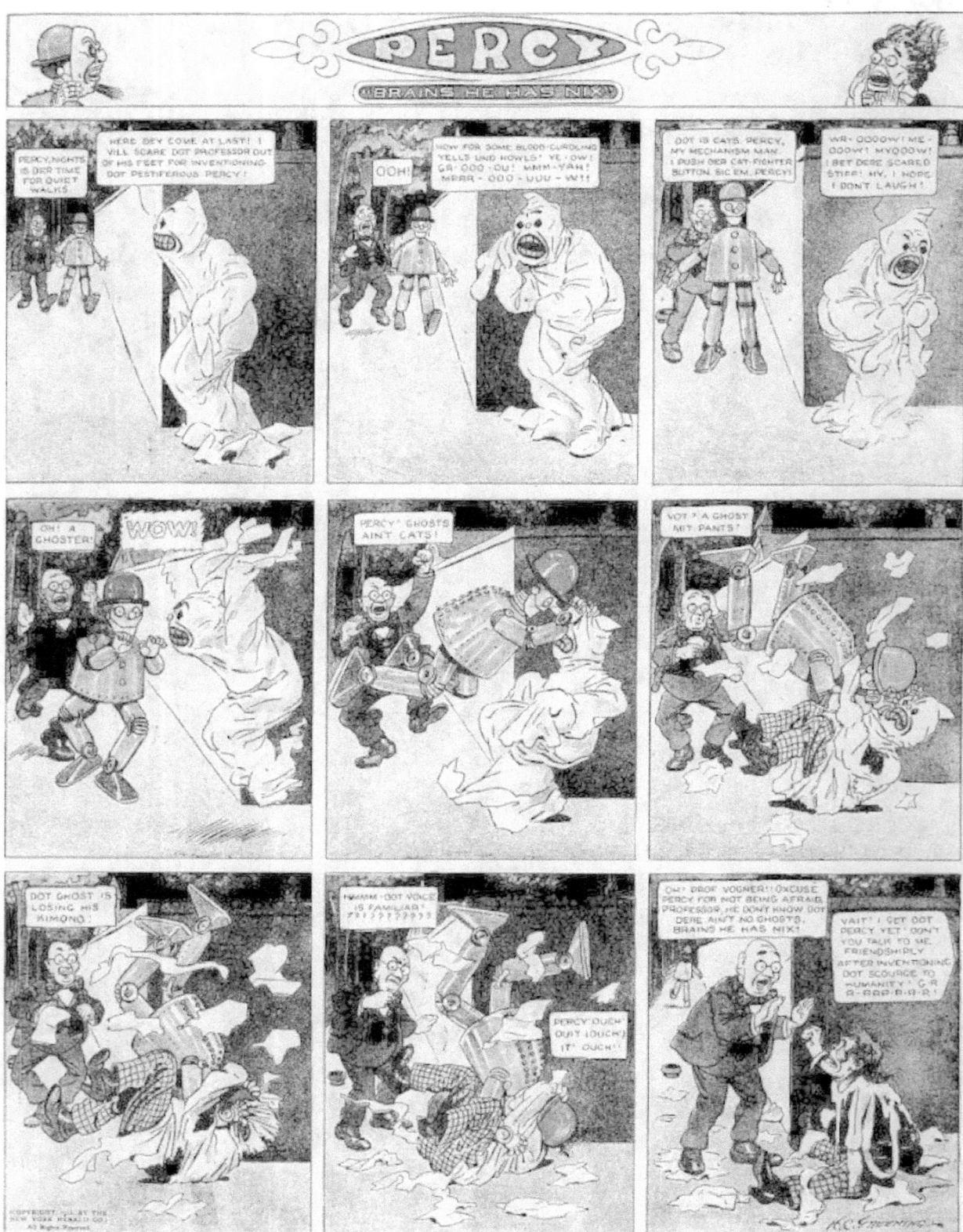

Percy: Brains He Has Nix by Harry Cornell Greening / Comic Strip #37 / Published in the Washington Evening Star June 9, 1912

44

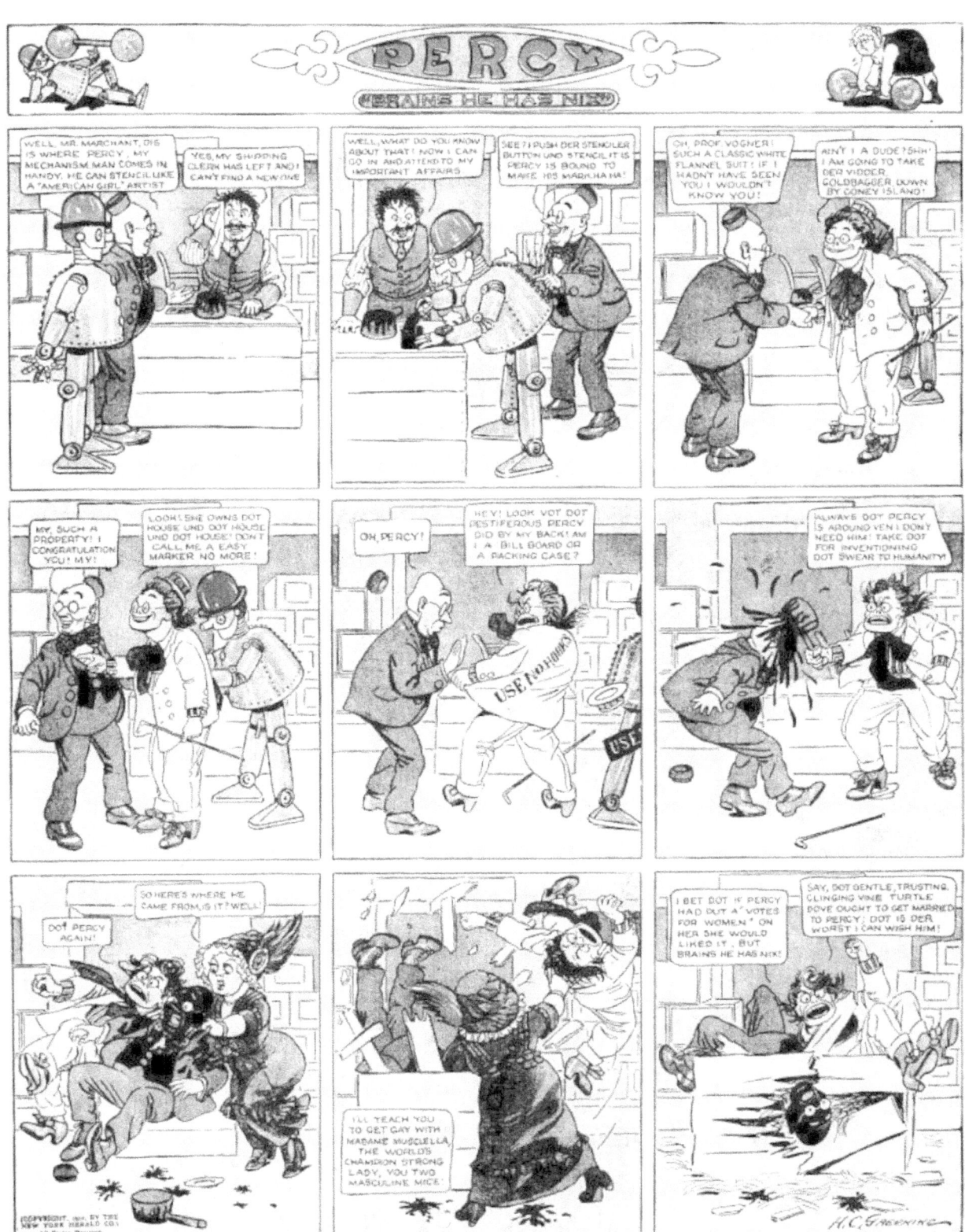

Percy: Brains He Has Nix by Harry Cornell Greening / Comic Strip #38 / Published in the Washington Evening Star June 16, 1912

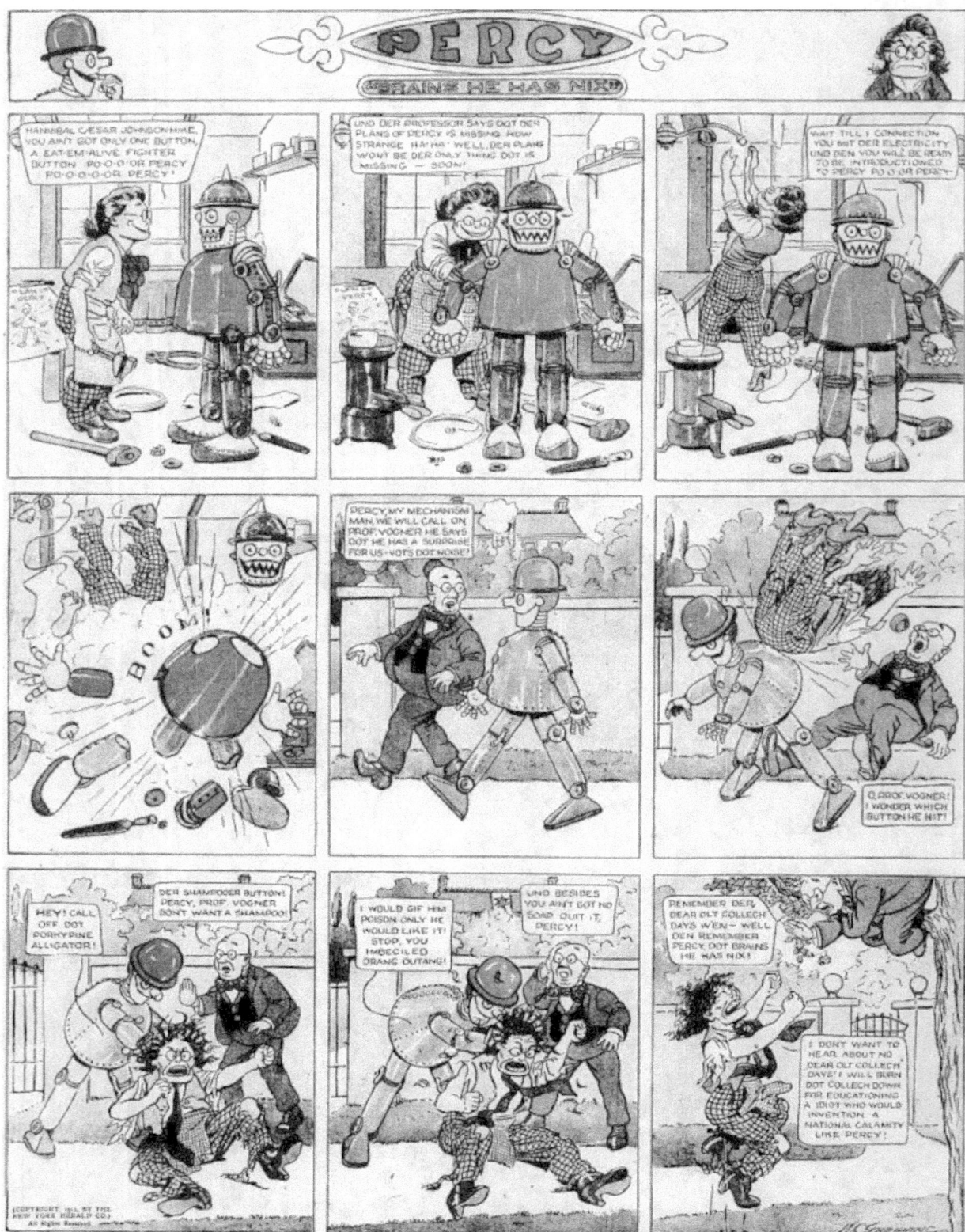

Percy: Brains He Has Nix by Harry Cornell Greening / Comic Strip #39 / Published in the Washington Evening Star June 23, 1912

46

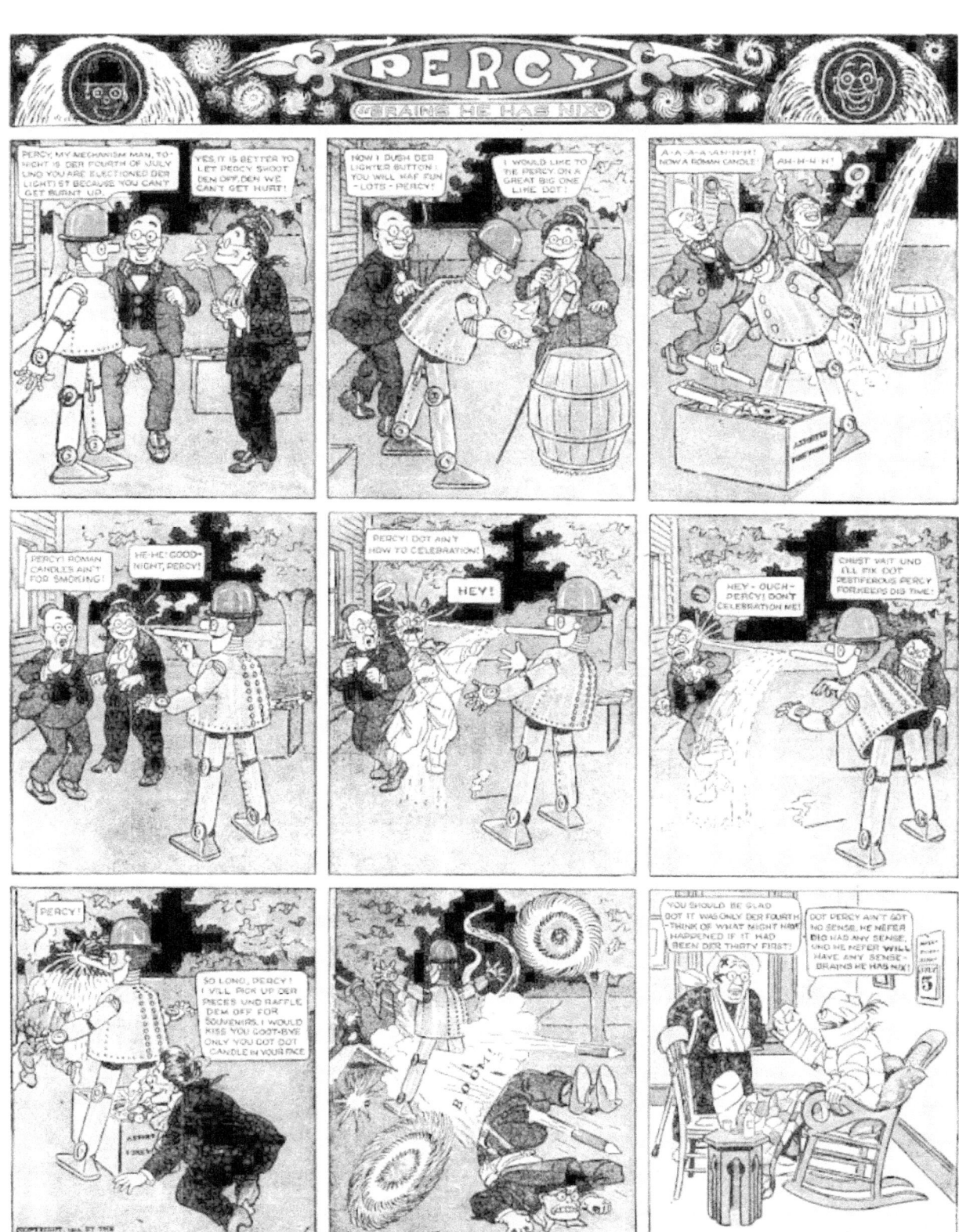

Percy: Brains He Has Nix by Harry Cornell Greening / Comic Strip #40 / Published in the Washington Evening Star June 30, 1912

47

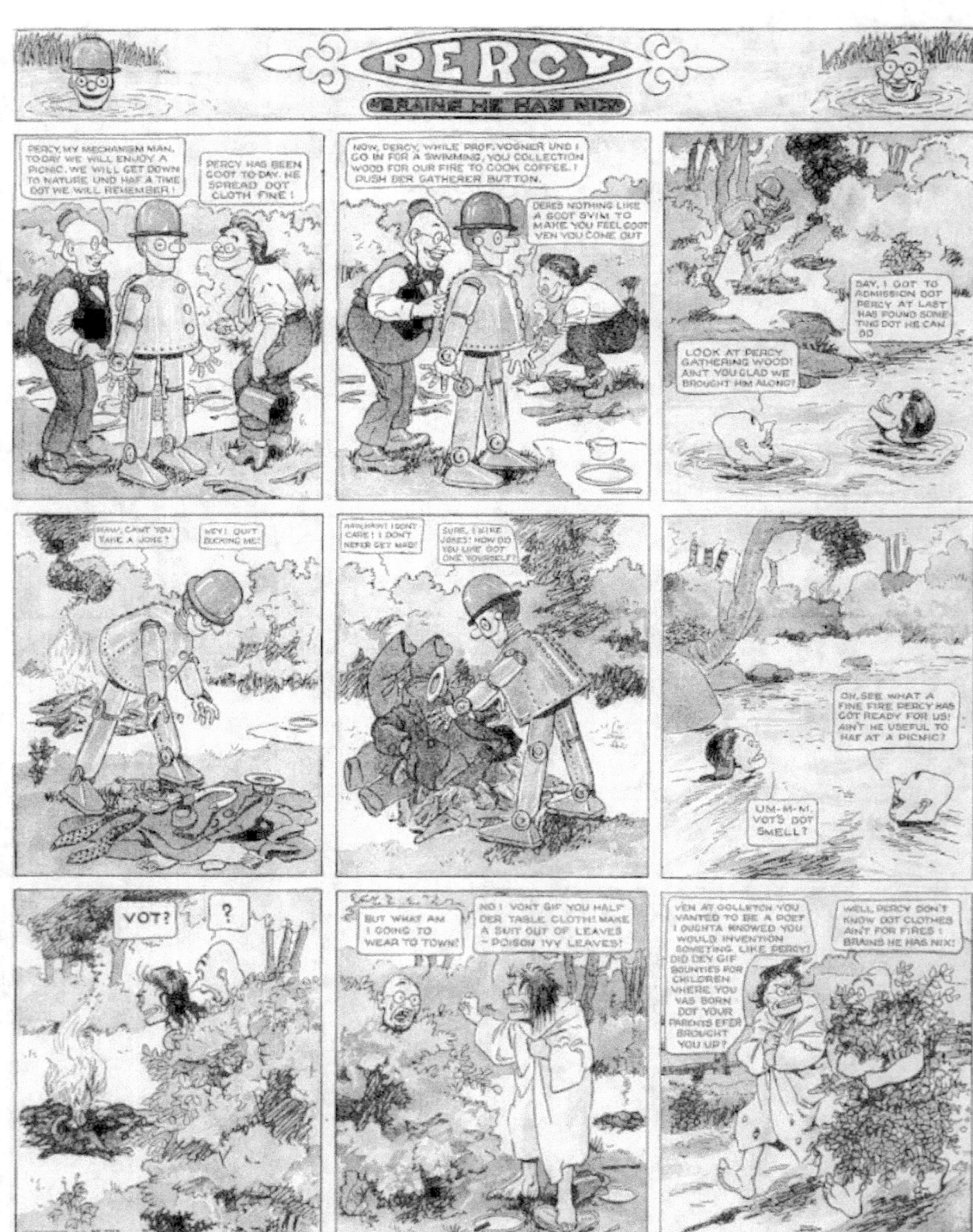

Percy: Brains He Has Nix by Harry Cornell Greening / Comic Strip #41 / Published in the Washington Evening Star July 7, 1912

48

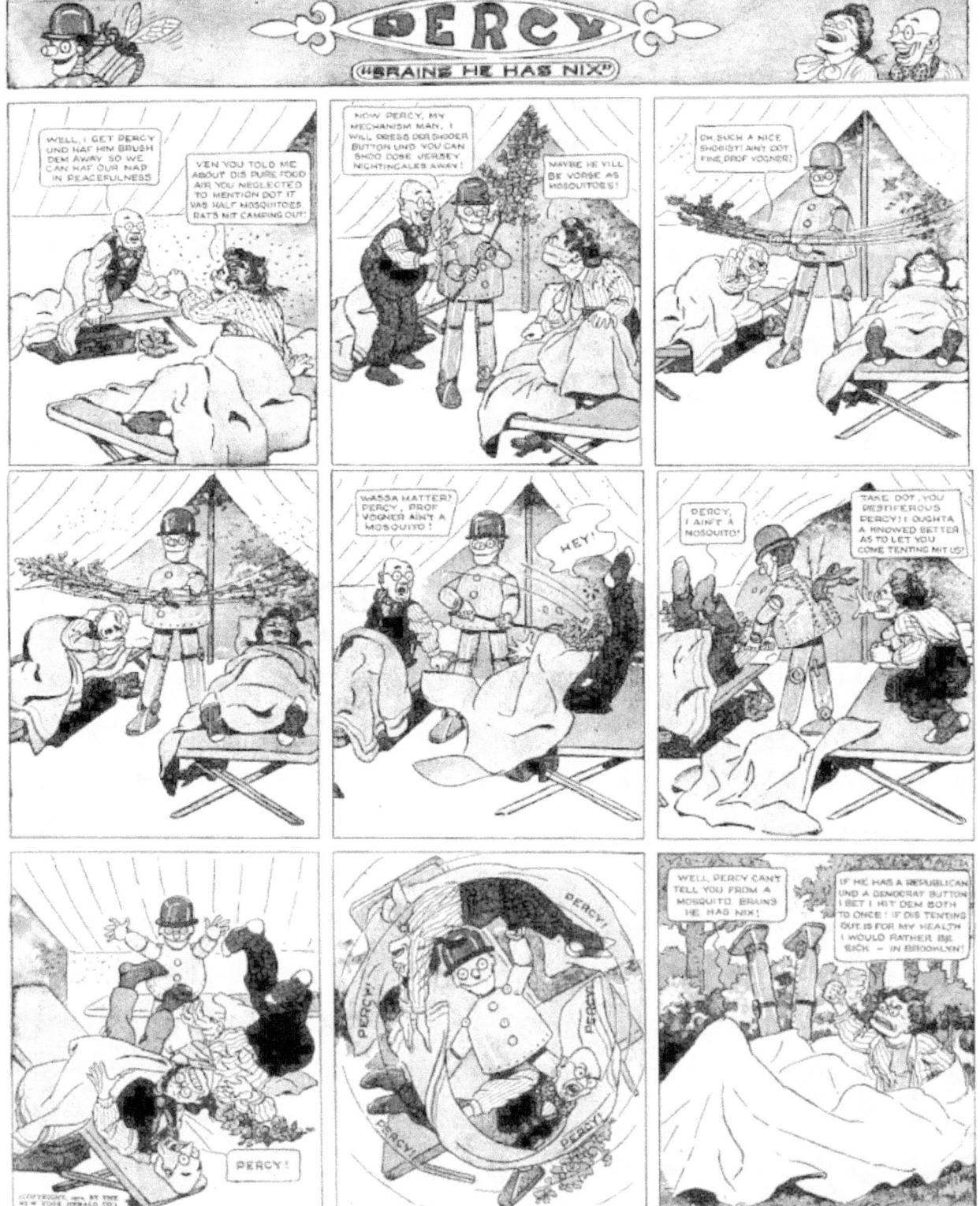

Percy: Brains He Has Nix by Harry Cornell Greening / Comic Strip #42 / Published in the Washington Evening Star July 14, 1912

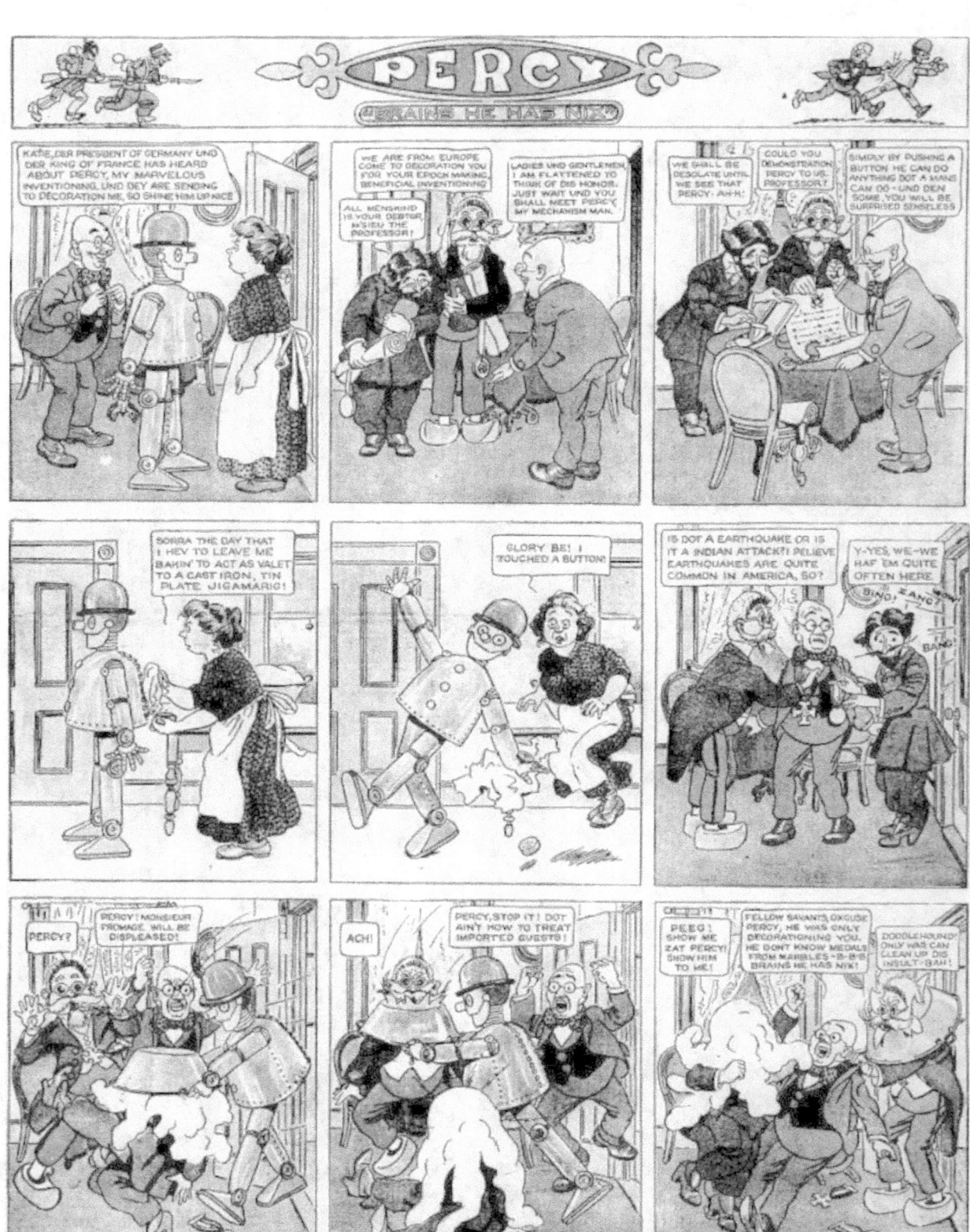

Percy: Brains He Has Nix by Harry Cornell Greening / Comic Strip #43 / Published in the Washington Evening Star July 21, 1912

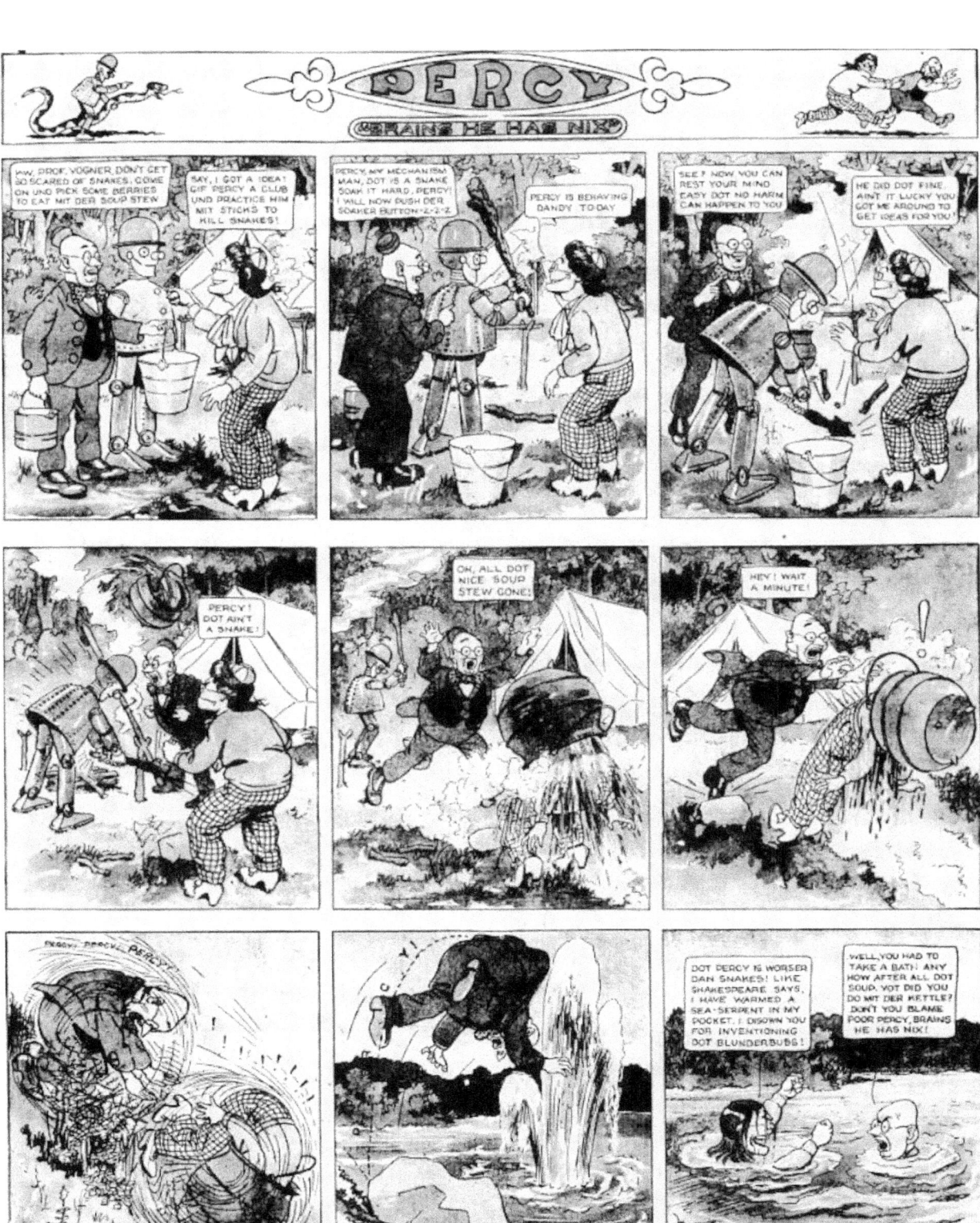

Percy: Brains He Has Nix by Harry Cornell Greening / Comic Strip #44 / Published in the Washington Evening Star July 28, 1912

51

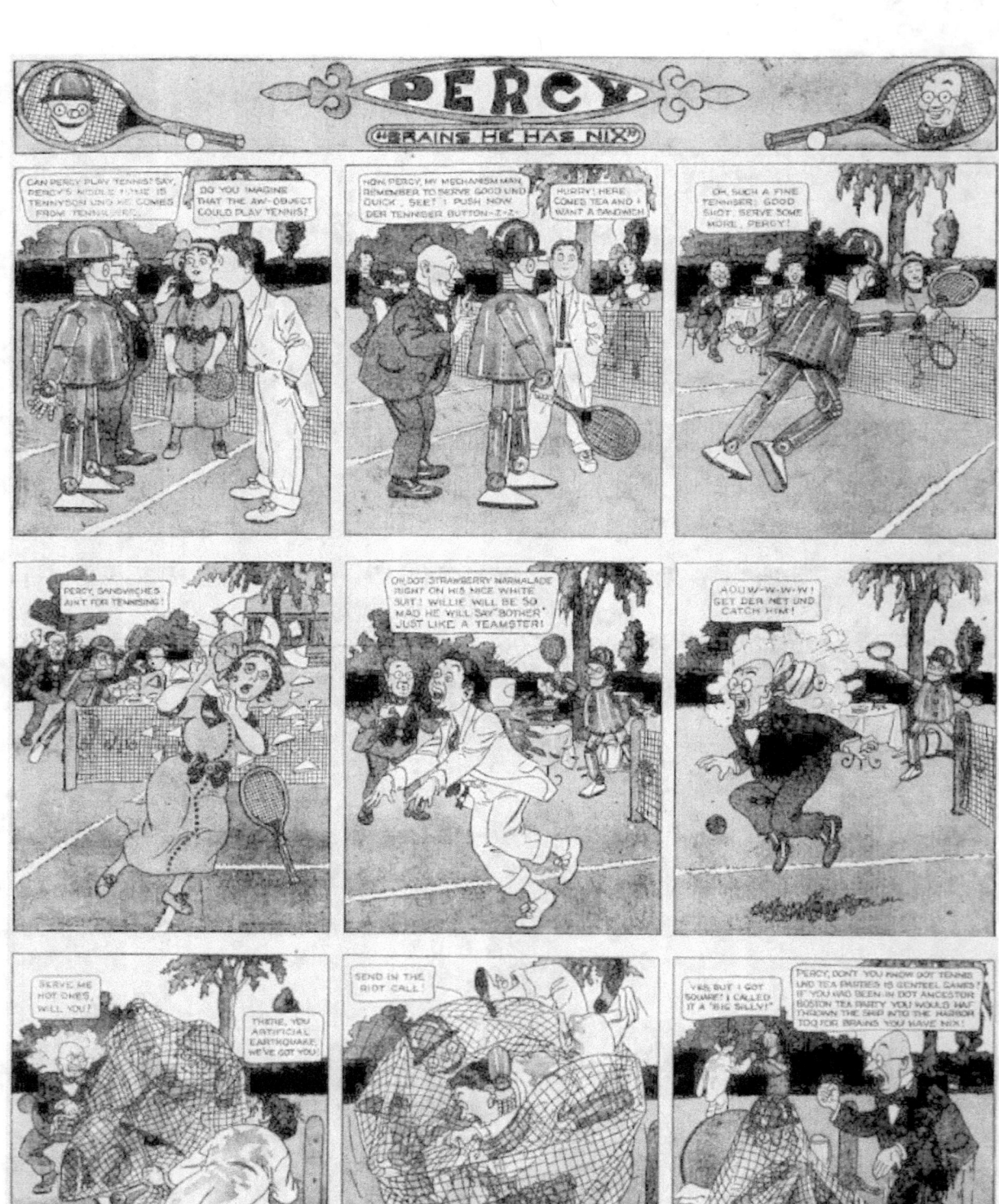

Percy: Brains He Has Nix by Harry Cornell Greening / Comic Strip #45 / Published in the Washington Evening Star August 4, 1912

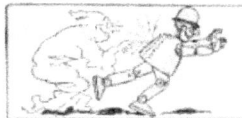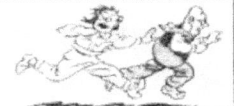

PERCY
"BRAINS HE HAS NIX"

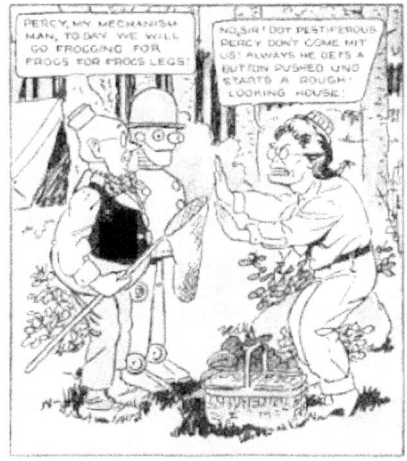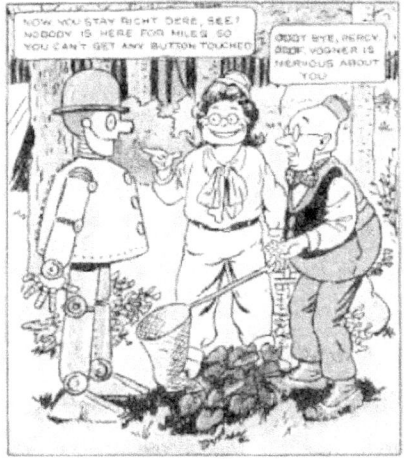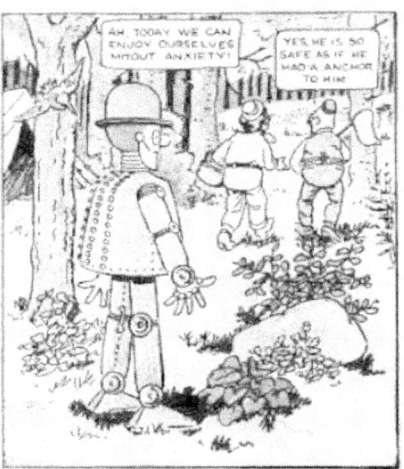

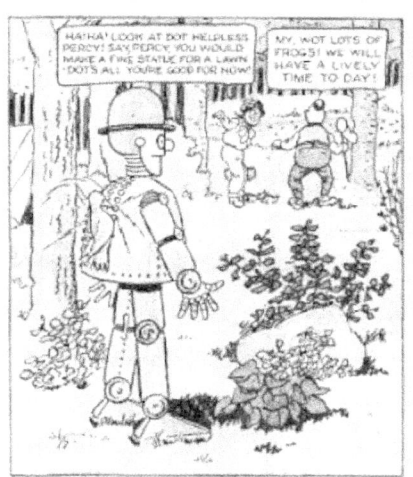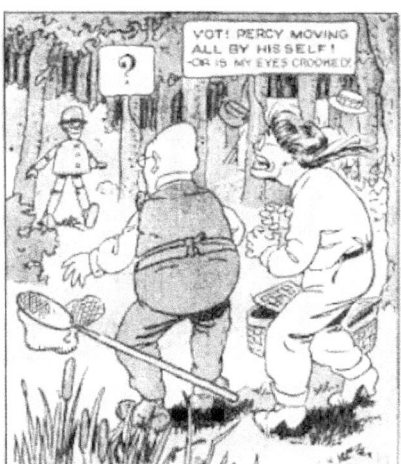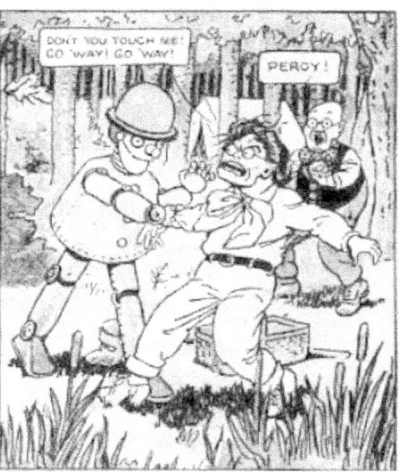

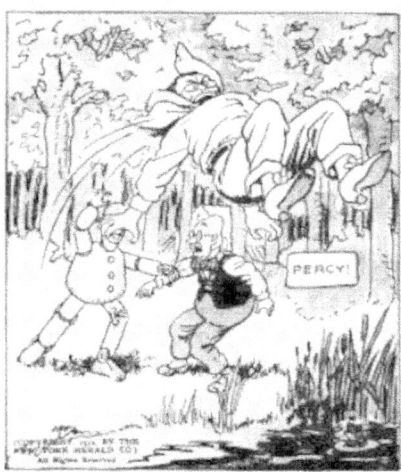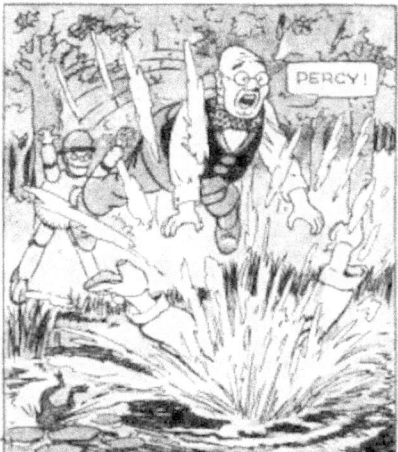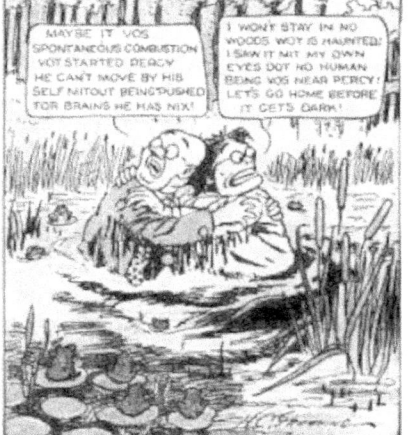

Percy: Brains He Has Nix by Harry Cornell Greening / Comic Strip #46 / Published in the Washington Evening Star Herald August 11, 1912

53

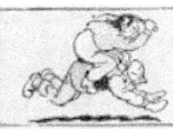
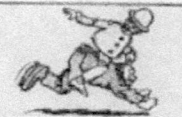

PERCY
"BRAINS HE HAS NIX"

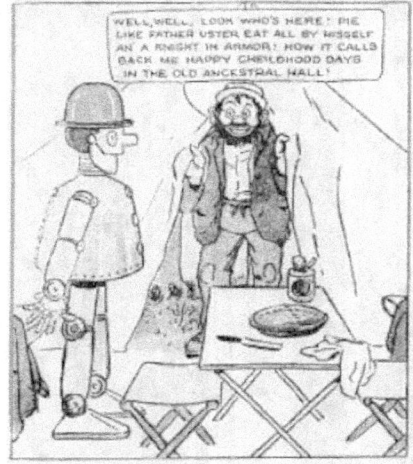
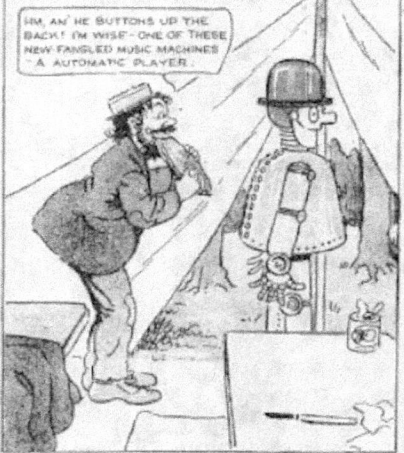
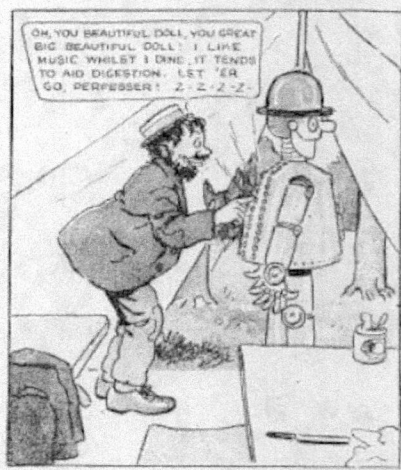
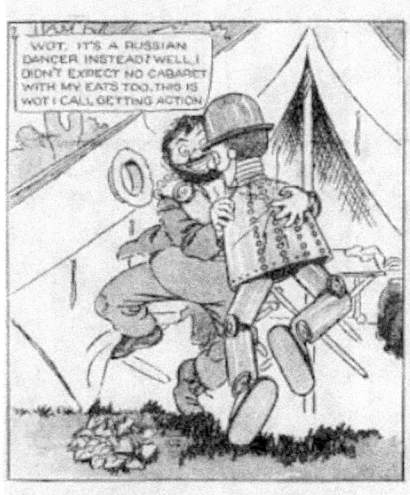
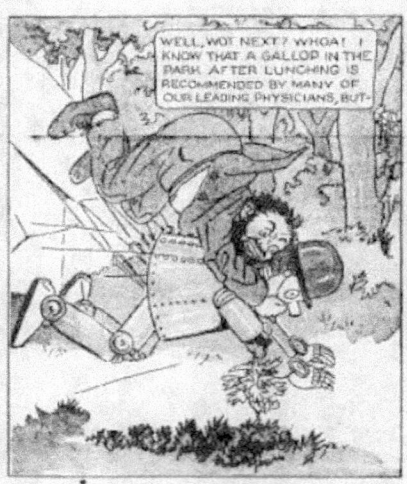
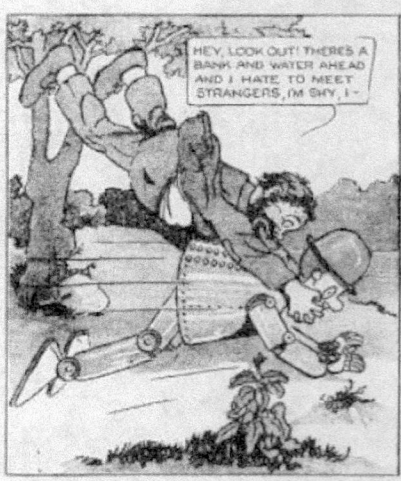
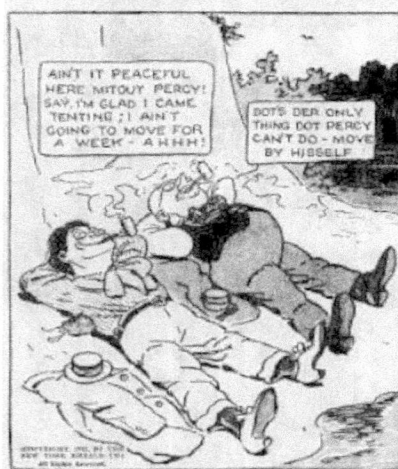
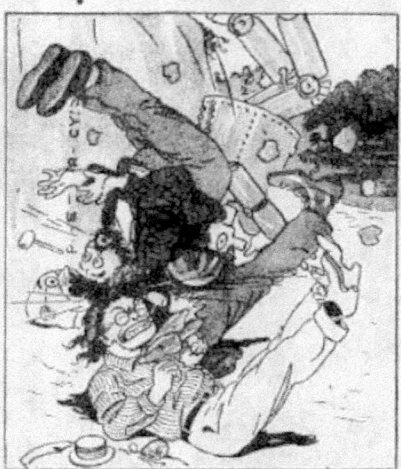
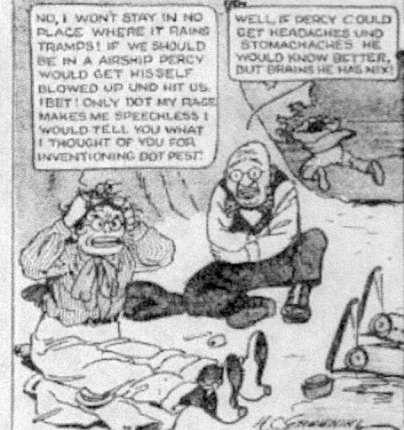

Percy: Brains He Has Nix by Harry Cornell Greening / Comic Strip #47 / Published in the Washington Evening Star August 11, 1912

54

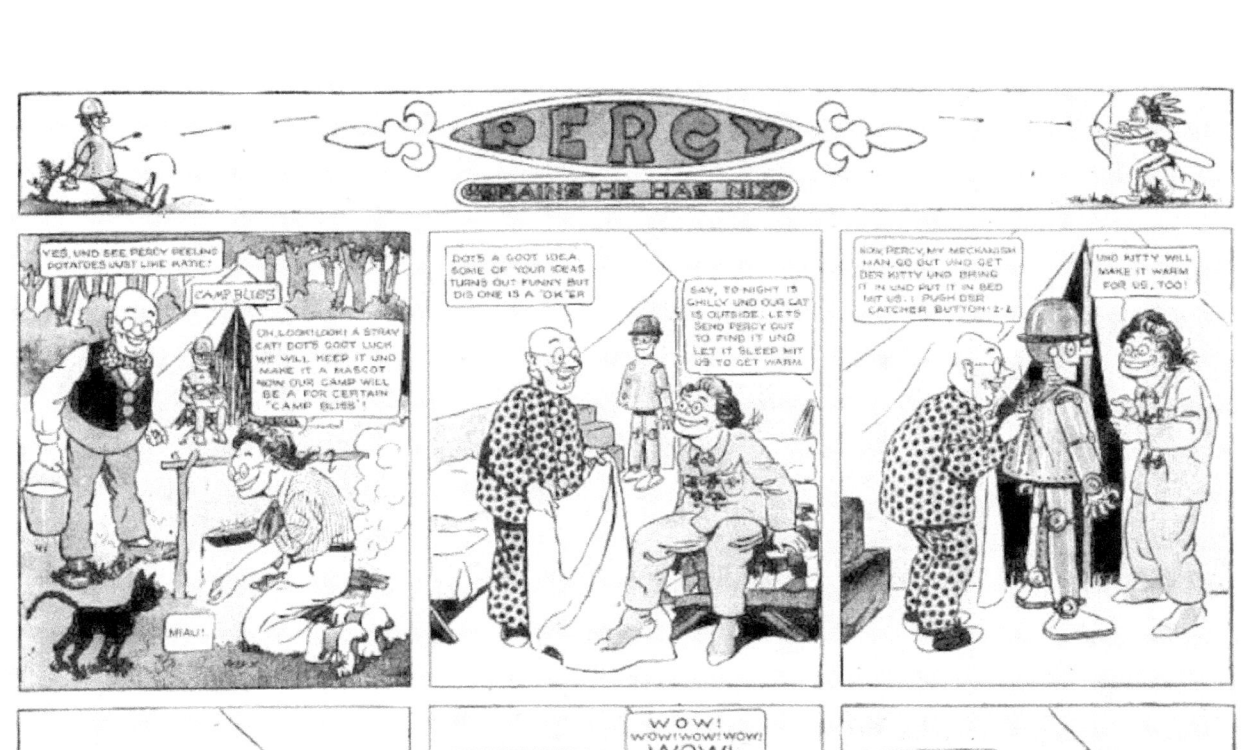

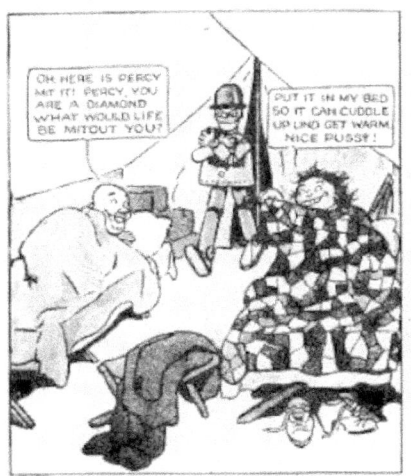
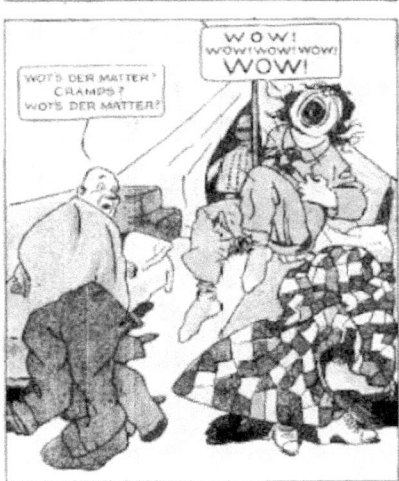
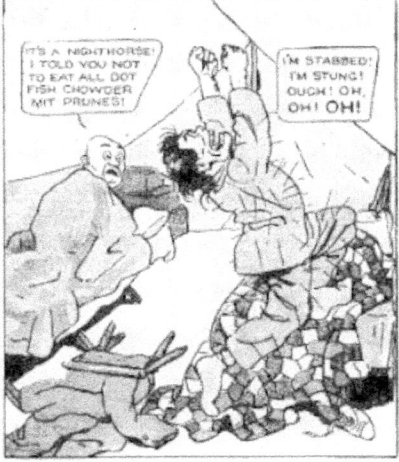

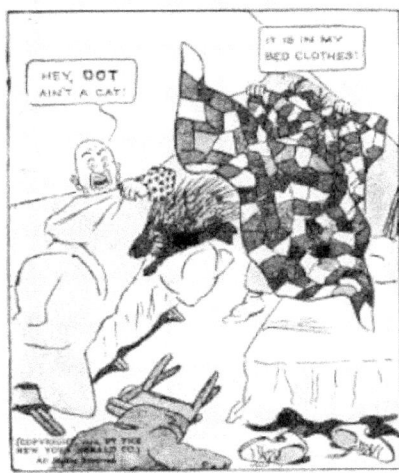
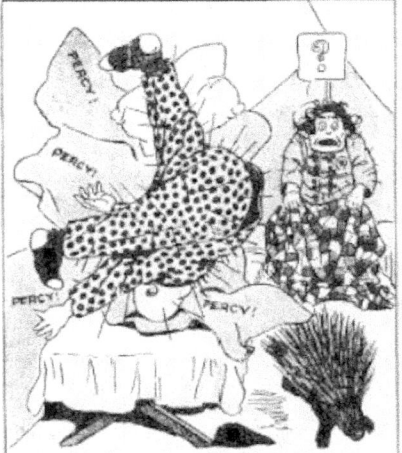
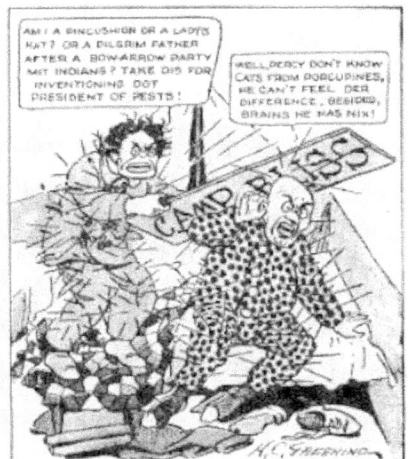

Percy: Brains He Has Nix by Harry Cornell Greening / Comic Strip #48 / Published in the Washington Evening Star August 18, 1912

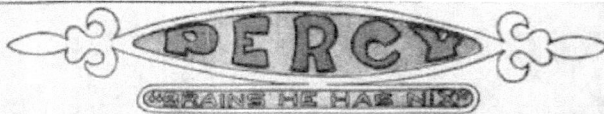
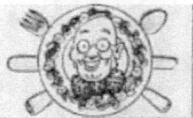

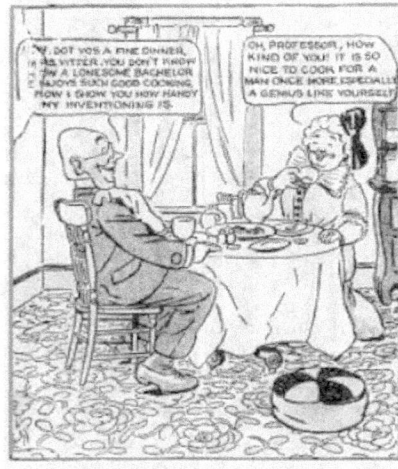
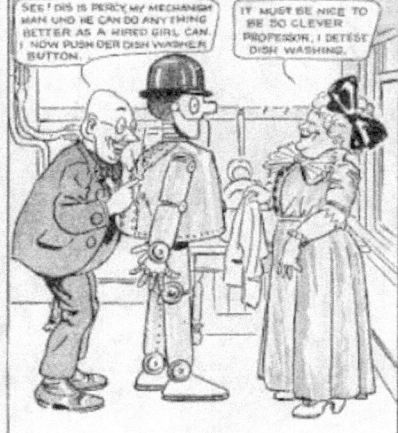
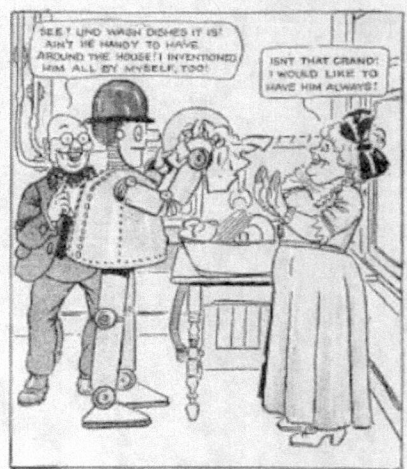

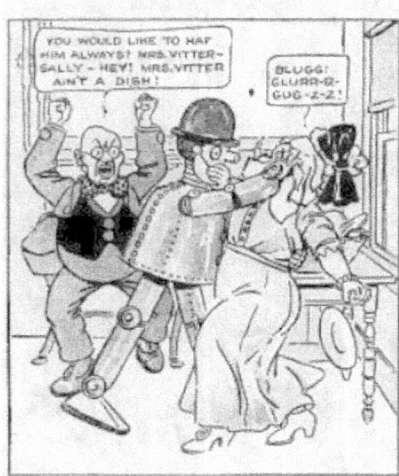
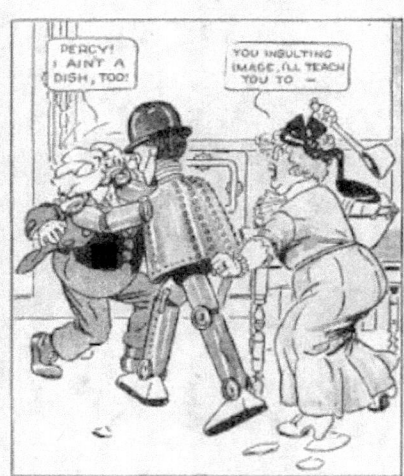
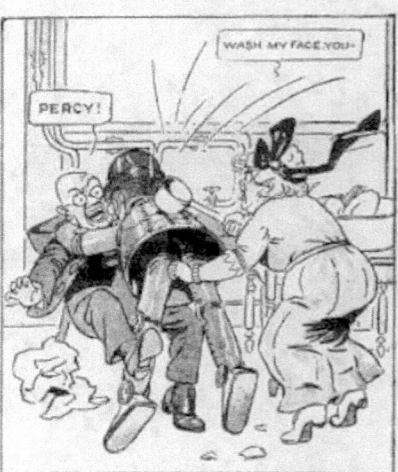

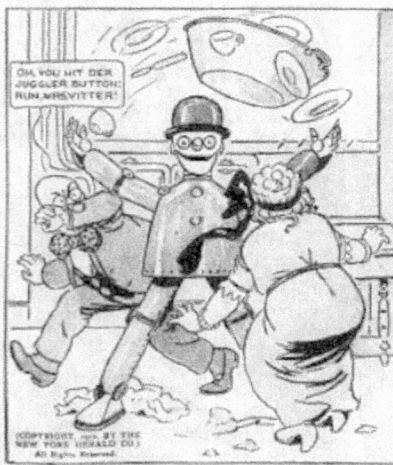
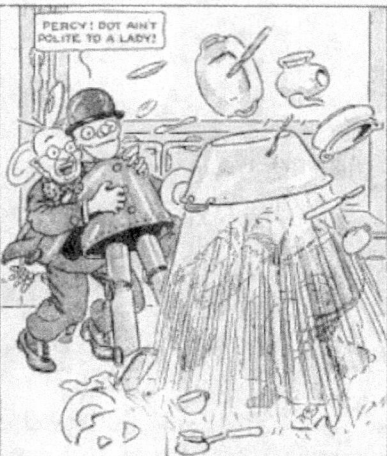
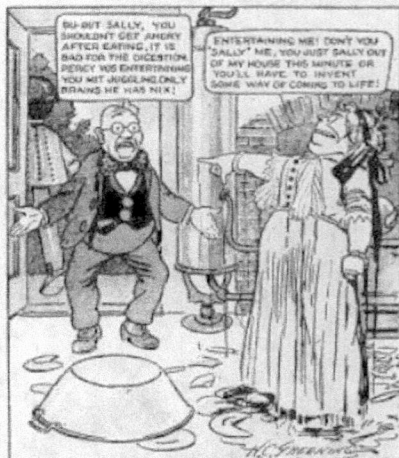

Percy: Brains He Has Nix by Harry Cornell Greening / Comic Strip #49 / Published in the Washington Evening Star August 25, 1912

56

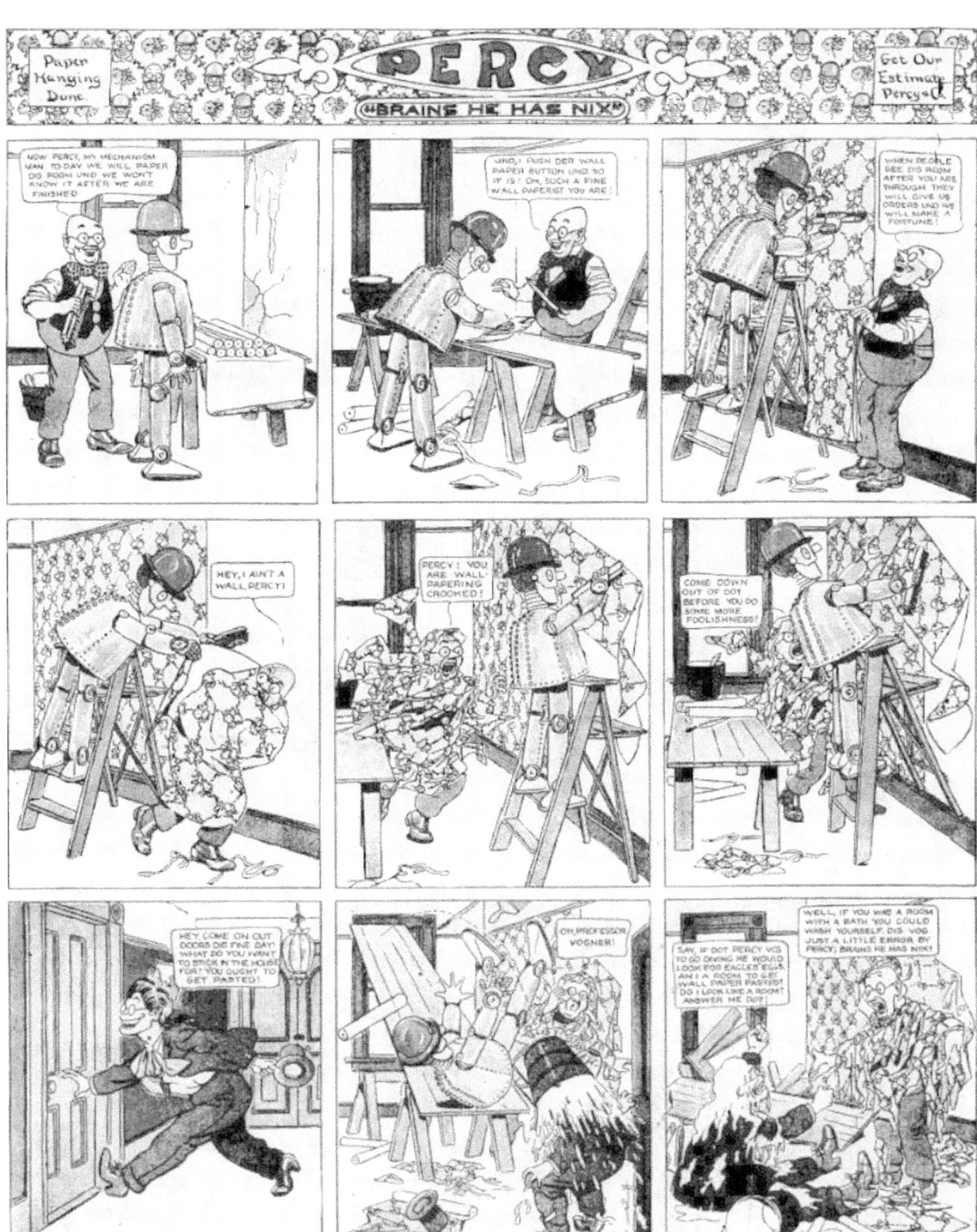

Percy: Brains He Has Nix by Harry Cornell Greening / Comic Strip #50 / Published in the Washington Evening Star September 1, 1912

57

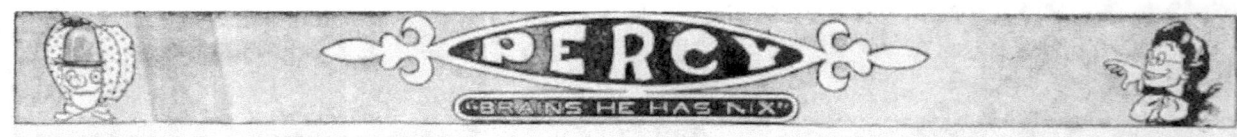

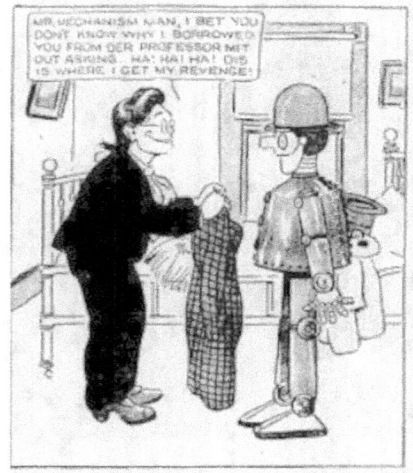
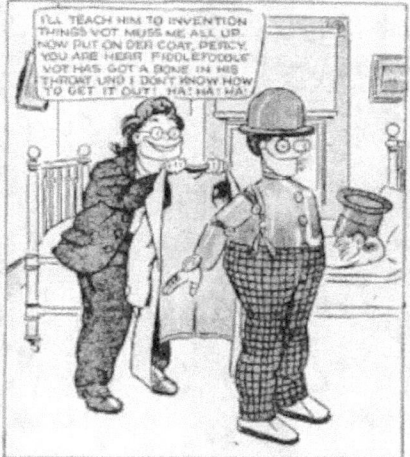
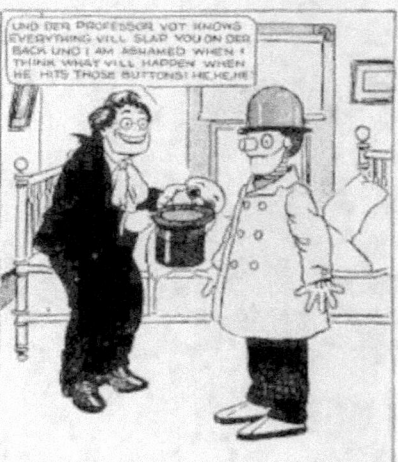

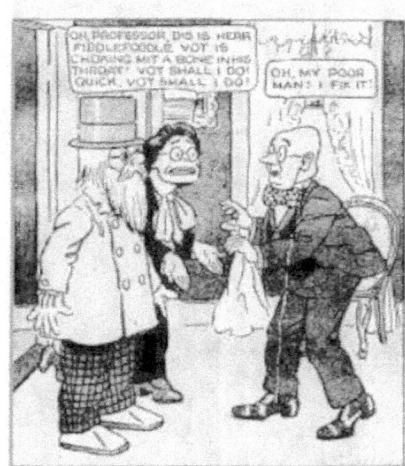
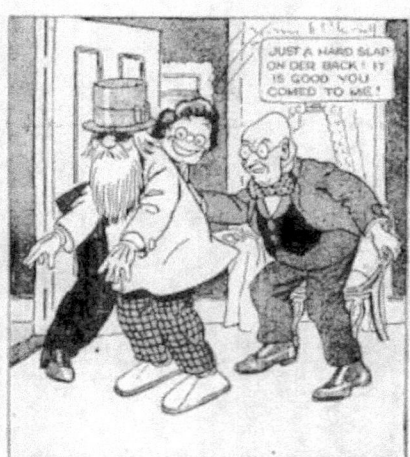
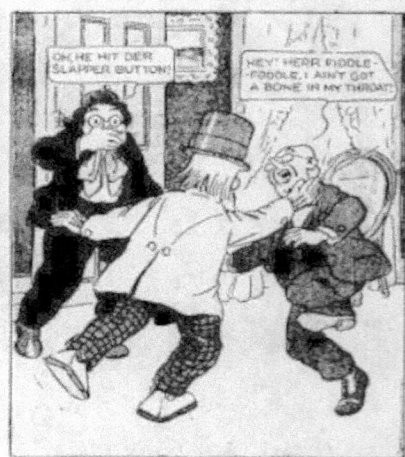

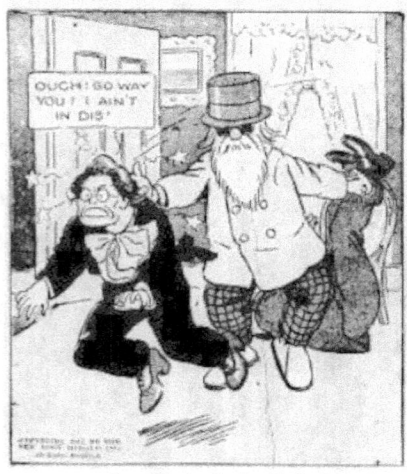
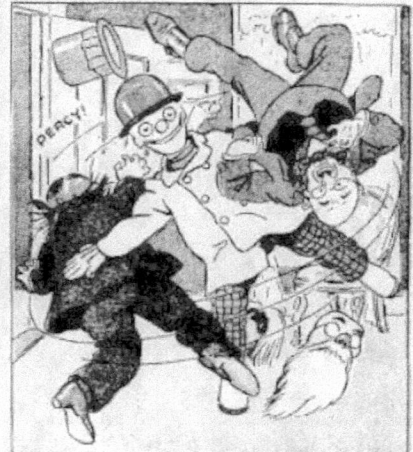
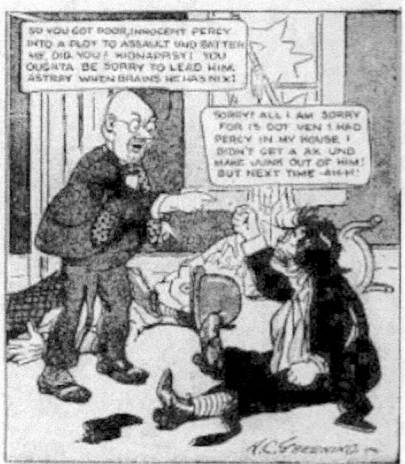

Percy: Brains He Has Nix by Harry Cornell Greening / Comic Strip #51 / PuPublished in the Washington Evening Star September 8, 1912

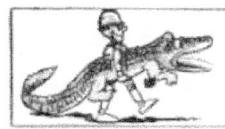
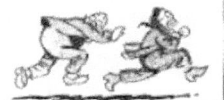

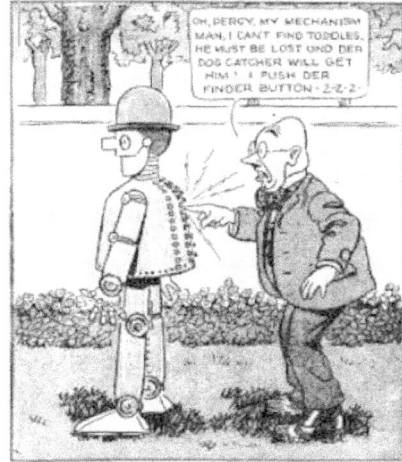
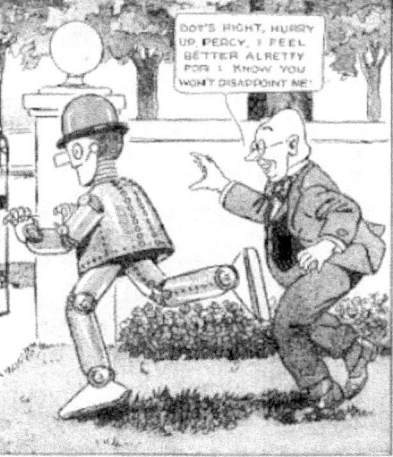
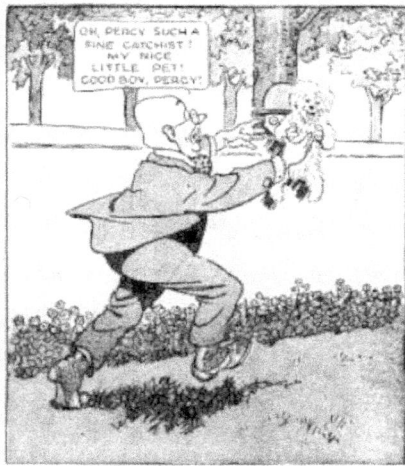
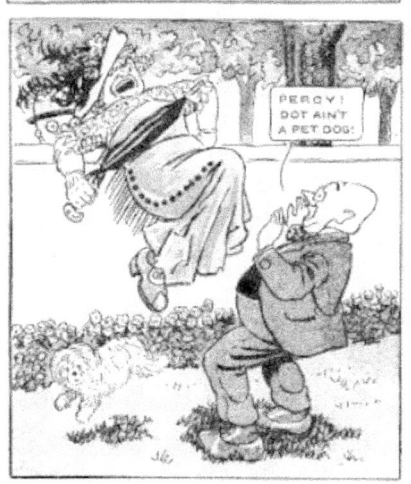
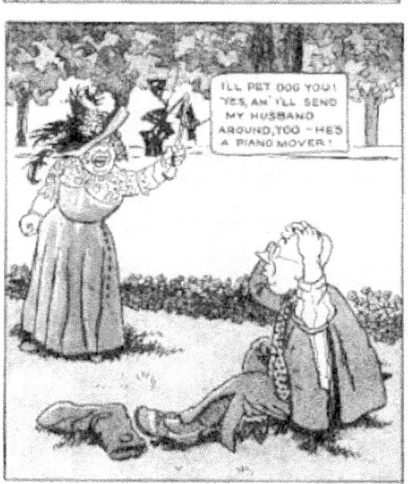
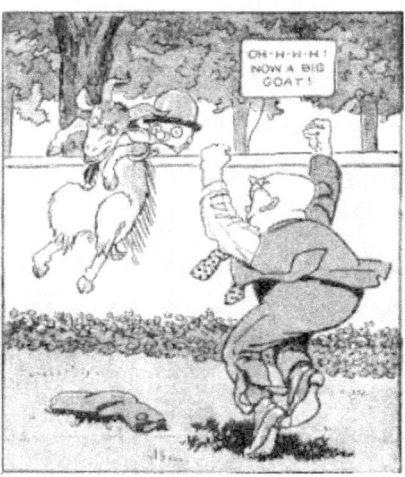
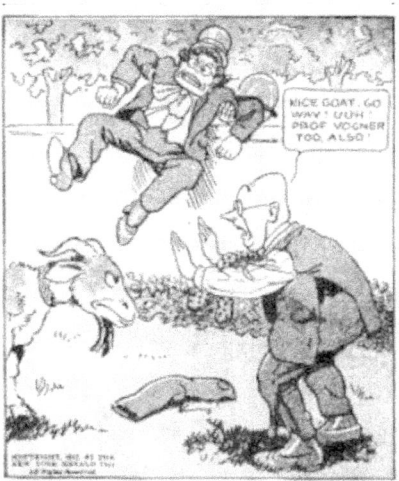
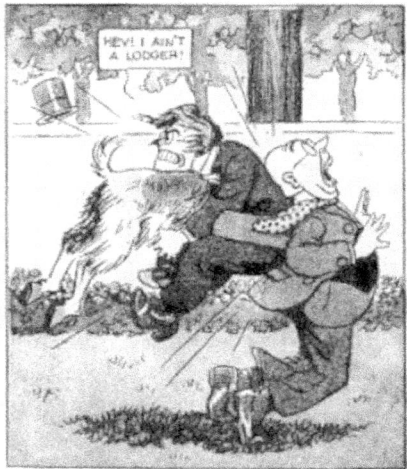
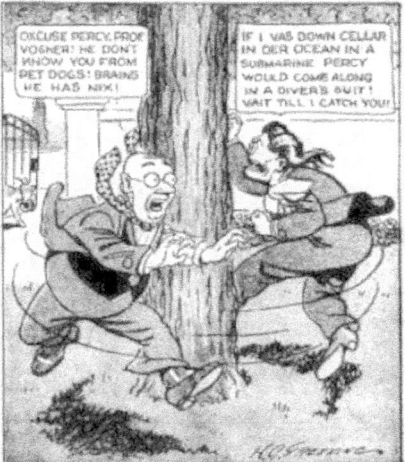

Percy: Brains He Has Nix by Harry Cornell Greening / Comic Strip #52 / Published in the Washington Evening Star September 15, 1912

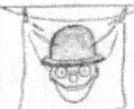
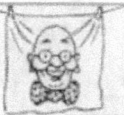

PERCY
BRAINS HE HAS NIX

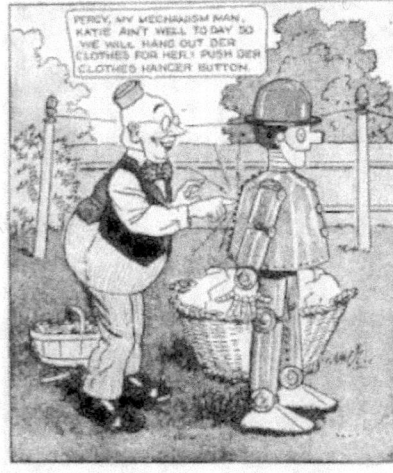
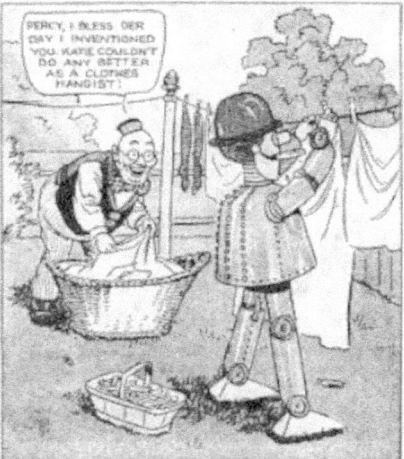
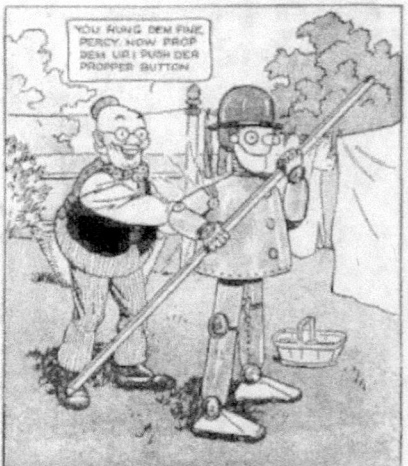

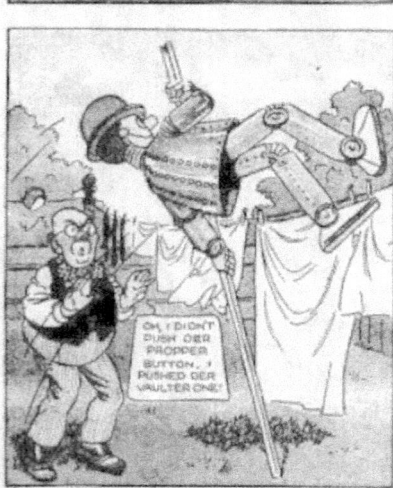
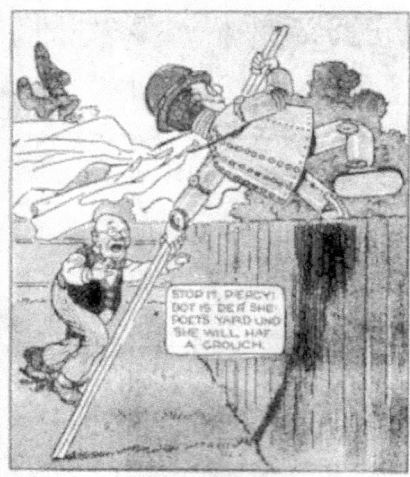
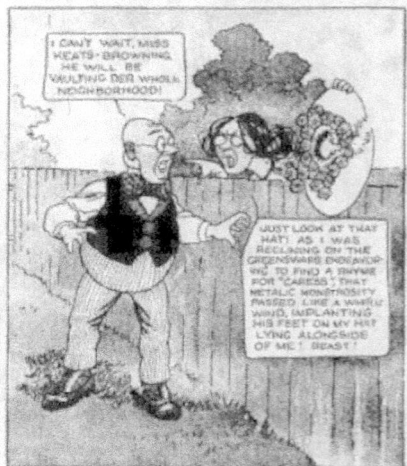

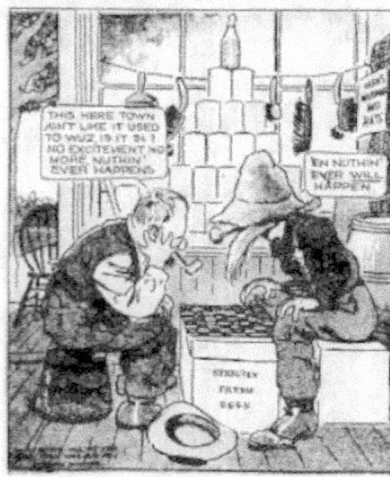
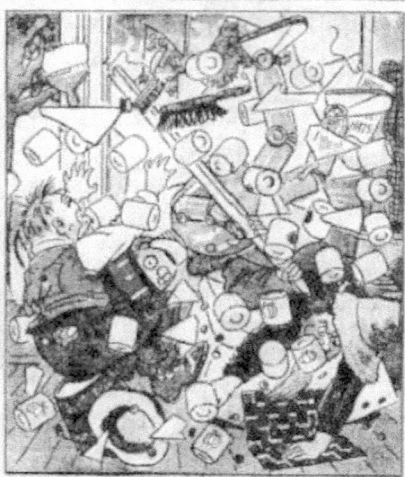
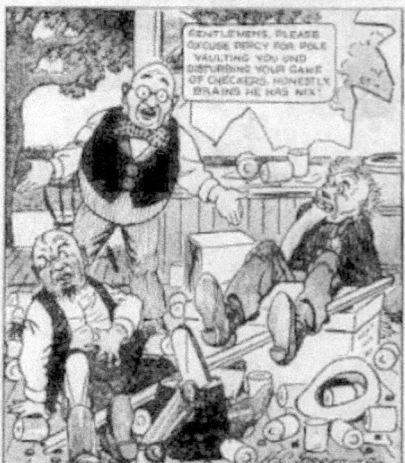

Percy: Brains He Has Nix by Harry Cornell Greening / Comic Strip #53 / Published in the Washington Evening Star September 22, 1912

60

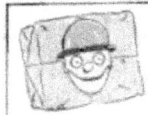
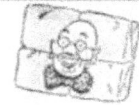
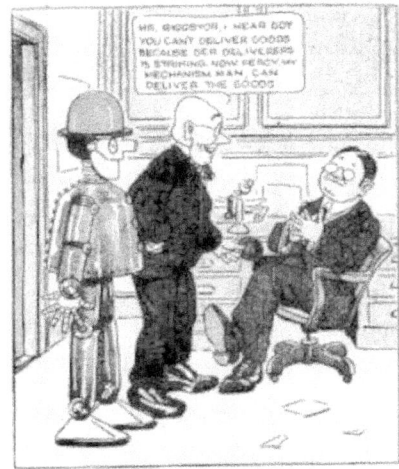
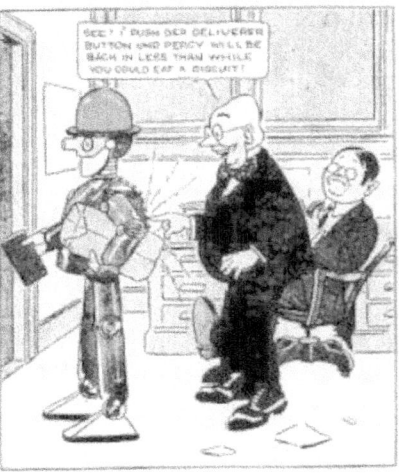
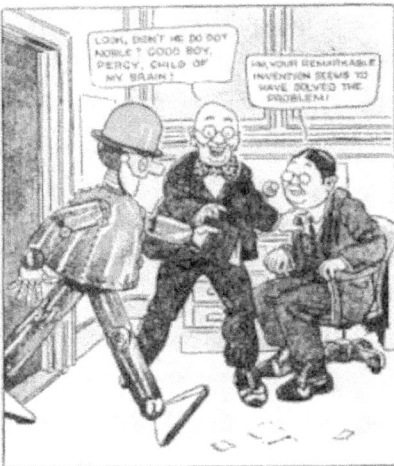
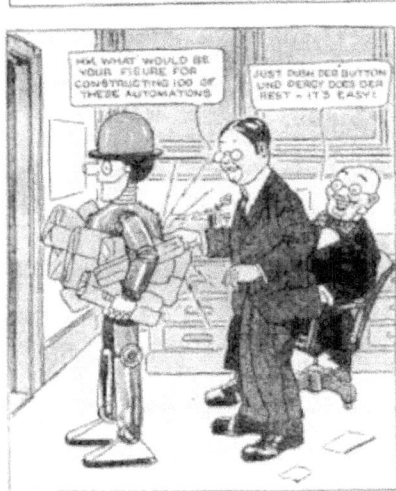
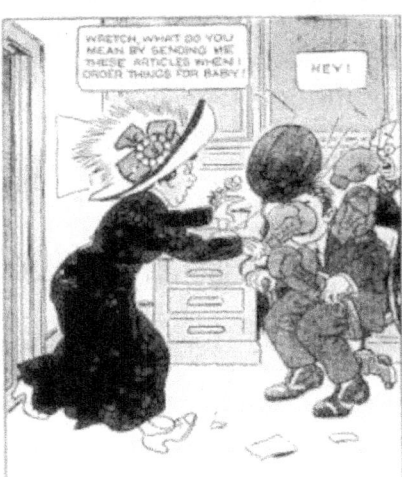
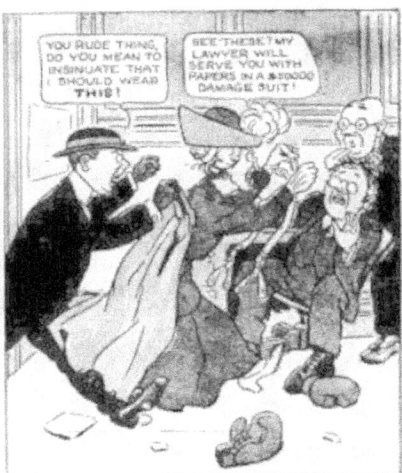
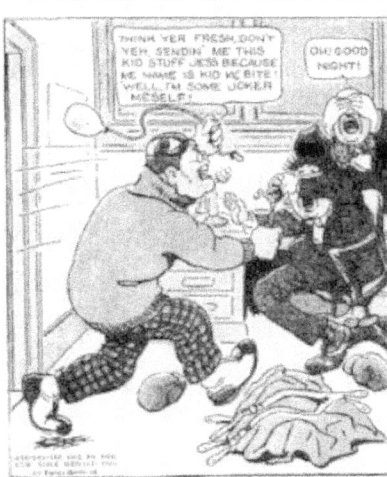
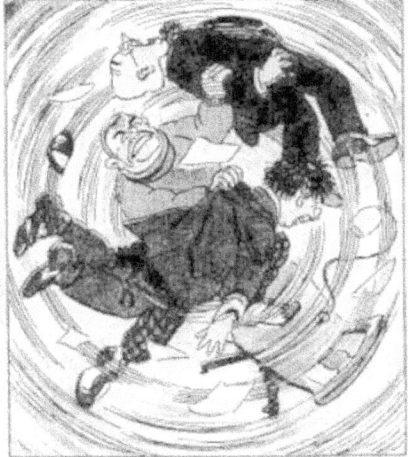
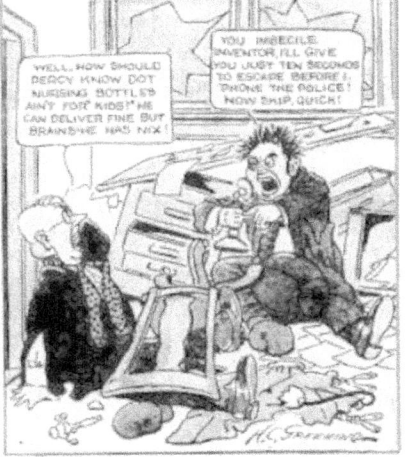

Percy: Brains He Has Nix by Harry Cornell Greening / Comic Strip #54 / Published in the Washington Evening Star September 29, 1912

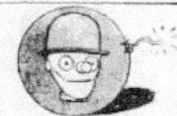
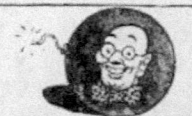

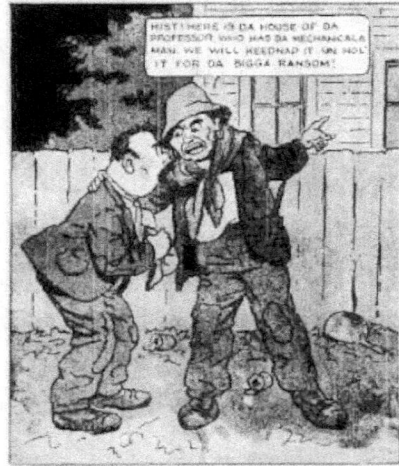
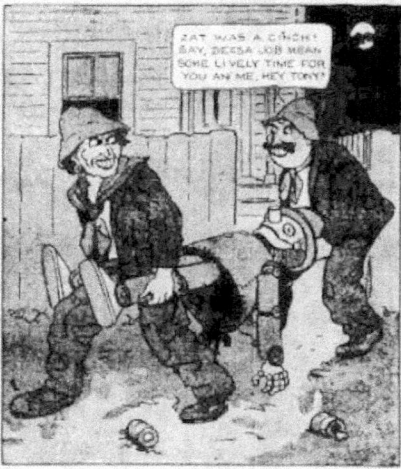
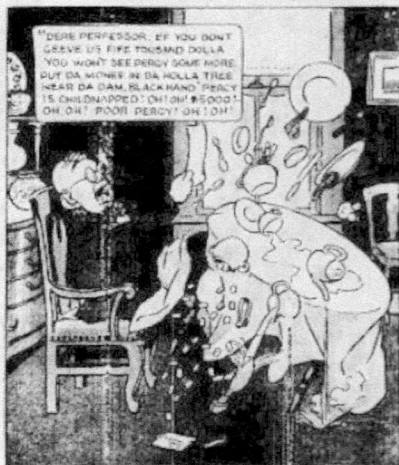
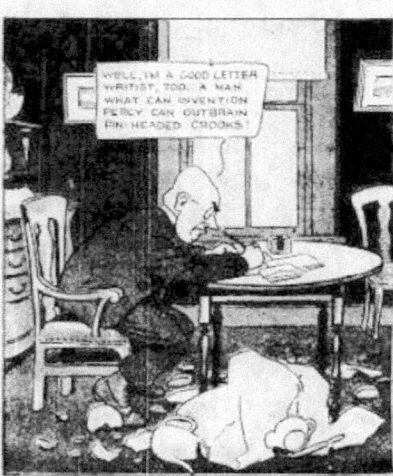
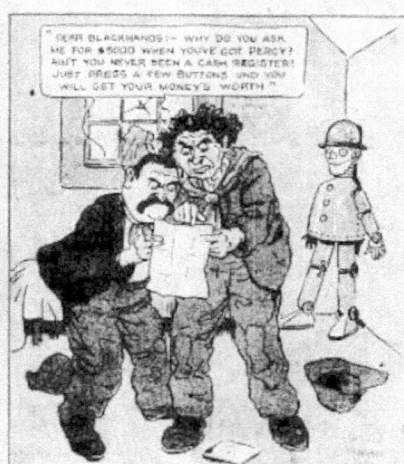
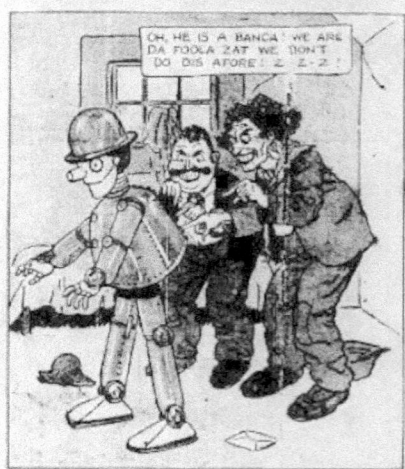
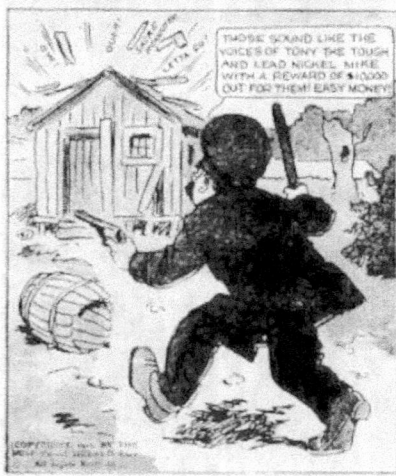
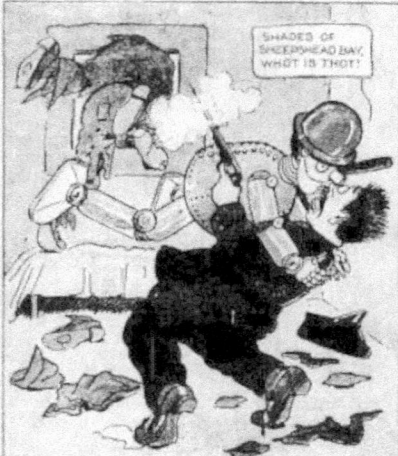
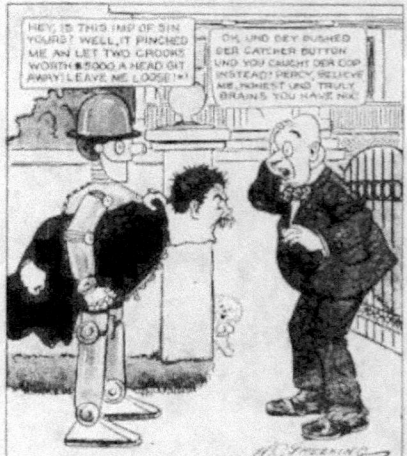

Percy: Brains He Has Nix by Harry Cornell Greening / Comic Strip #55 / Published in the Washington Evening Star October 6, 1912

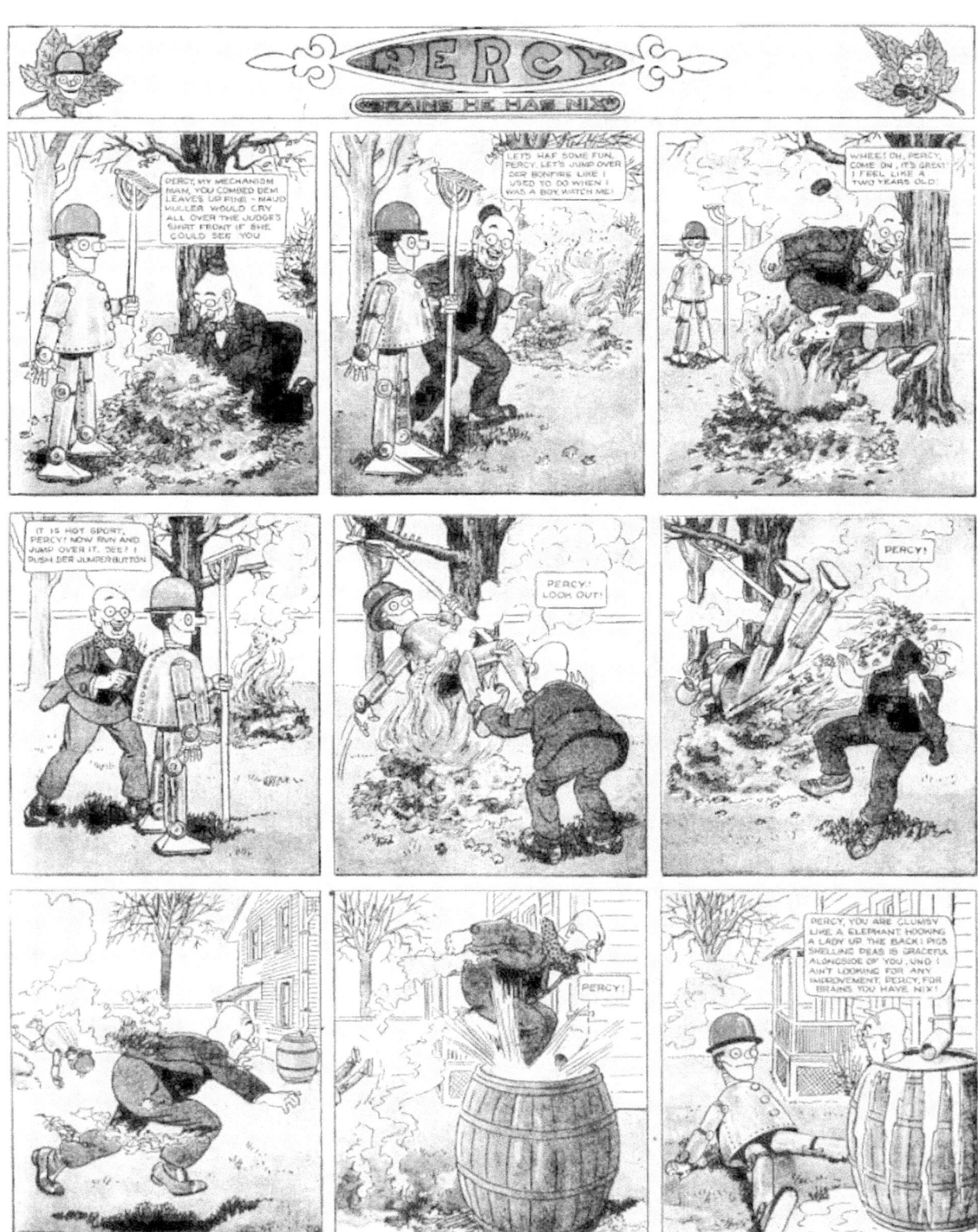

Percy: Brains He Has Nix by Harry Cornell Greening / Comic Strip #56 / Published in the Washington Evening Star October 13, 1912

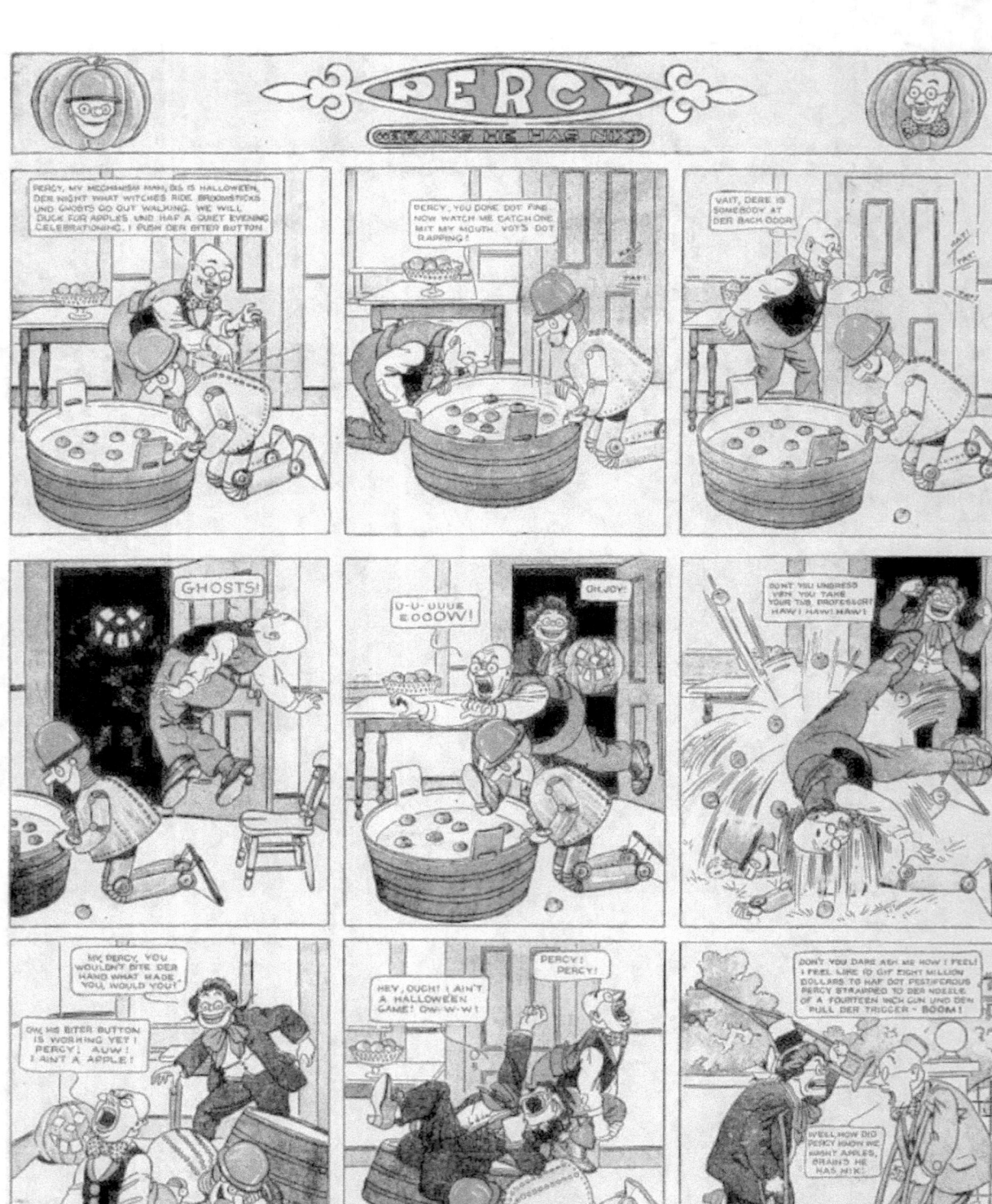

Percy: Brains He Has Nix by Harry Cornell Greening / Comic Strip #57 / Published in the Washington Evening Star October 20, 1912

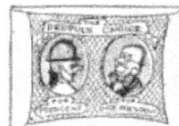
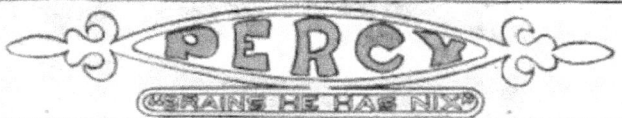

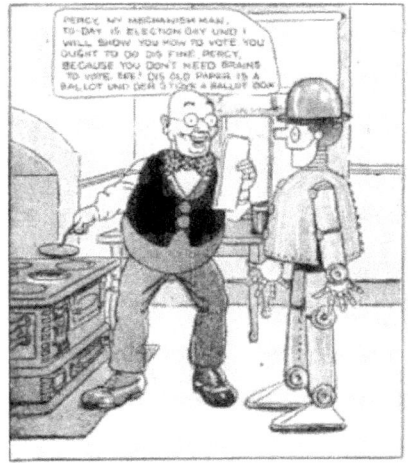
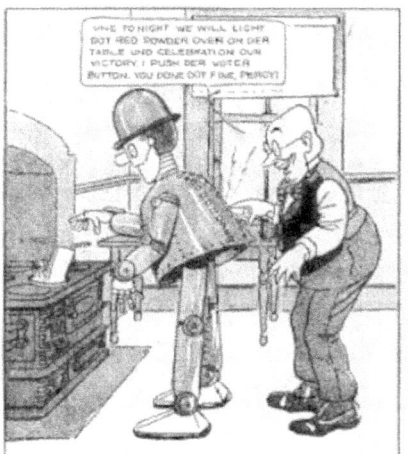
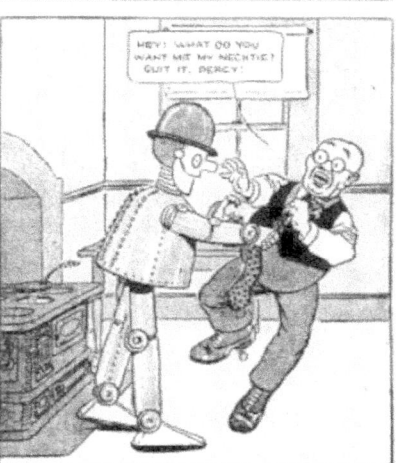

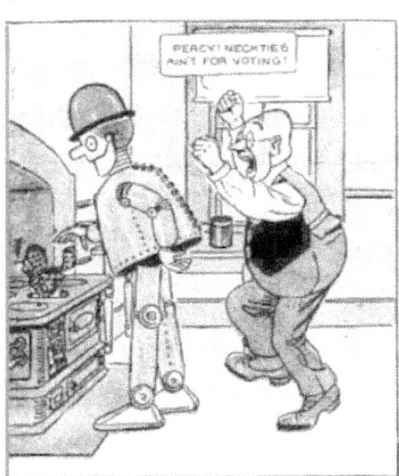
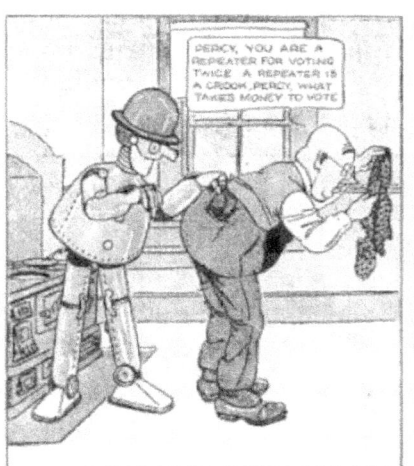
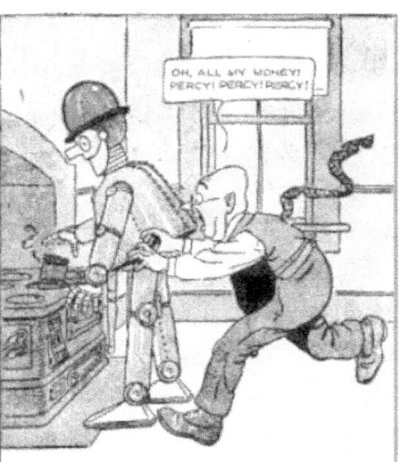

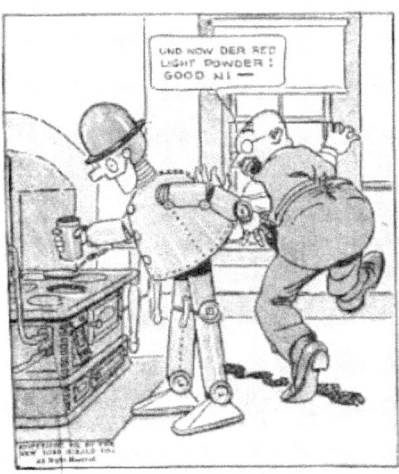
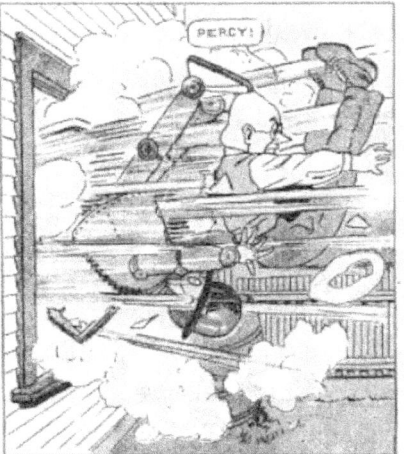
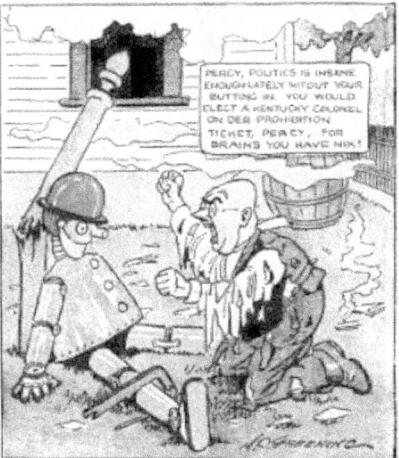

Percy: Brains He Has Nix by Harry Cornell Greening / Comic Strip #58 / Published in the Washington Evening Star October 27, 1912

65

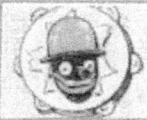
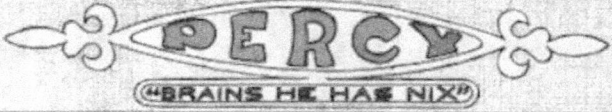
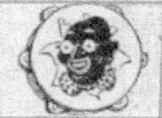

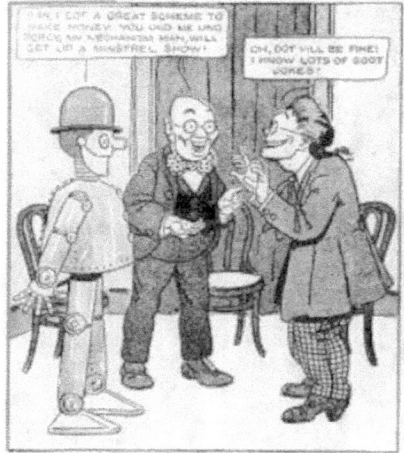
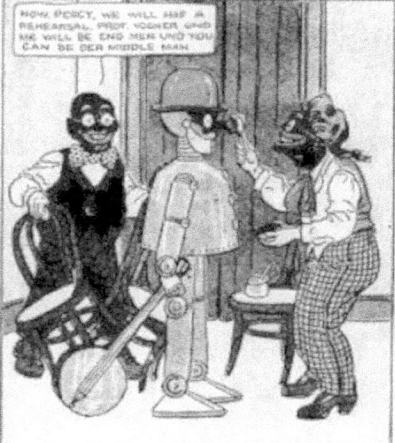
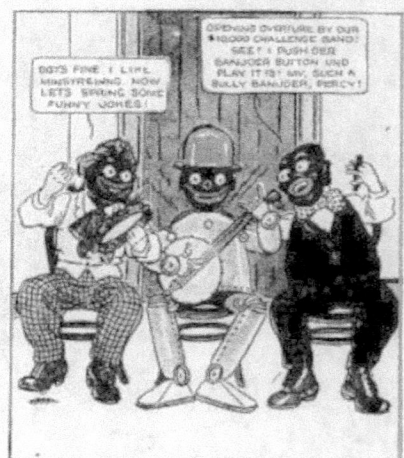

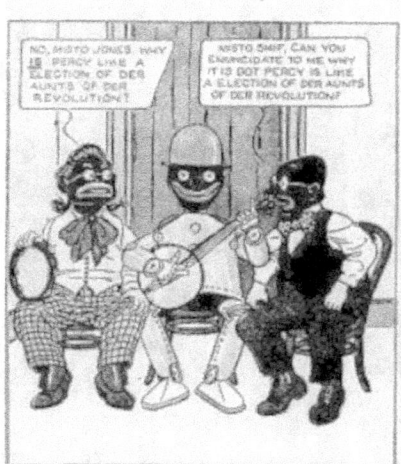
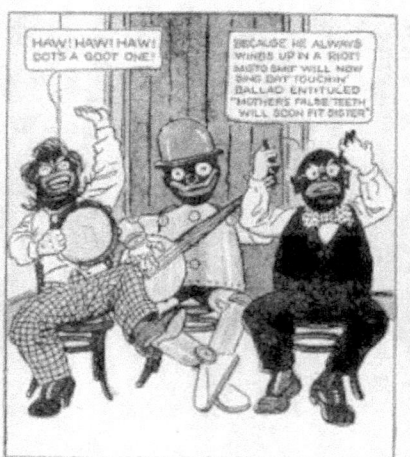
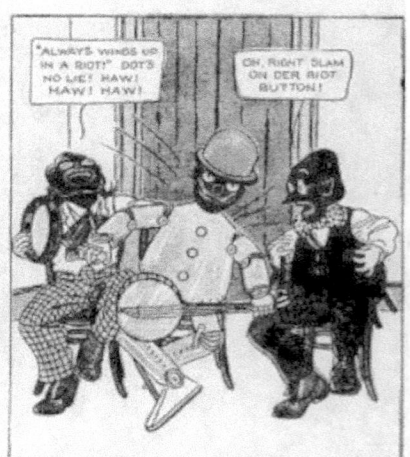

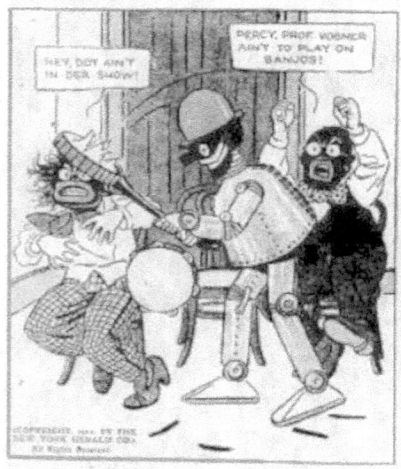
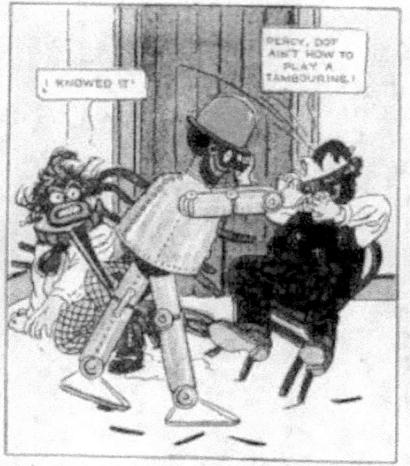
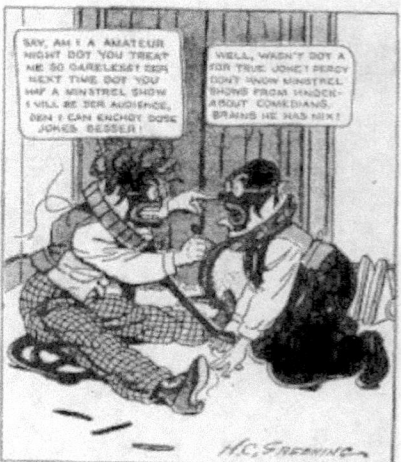

Percy: Brains He Has Nix by Harry Cornell Greening / Comic Strip #59 / Published in the Washington Evening Star November 3, 1912

66

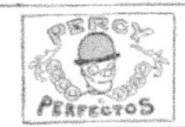
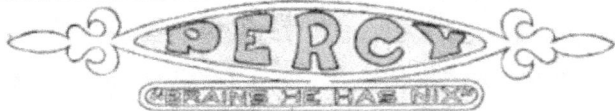
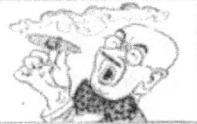

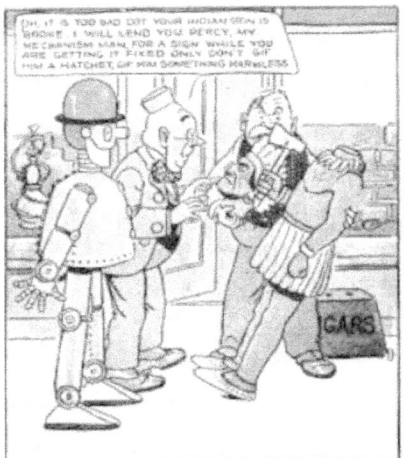
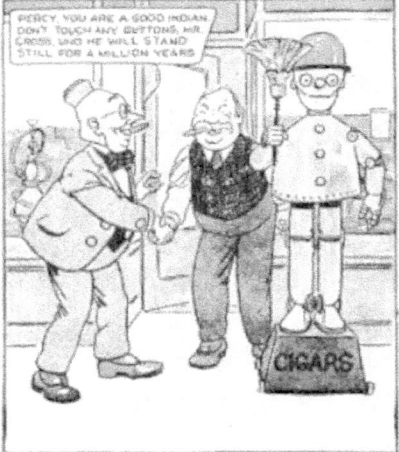
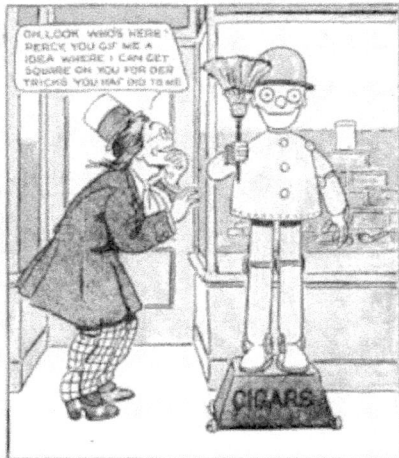

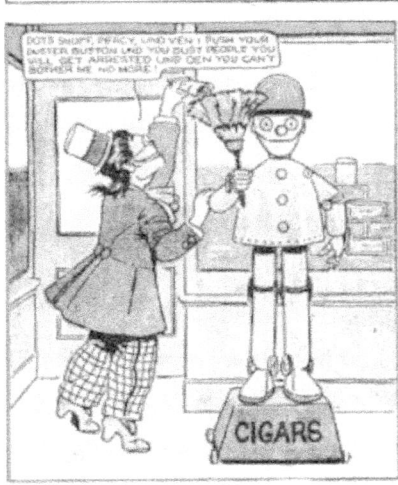
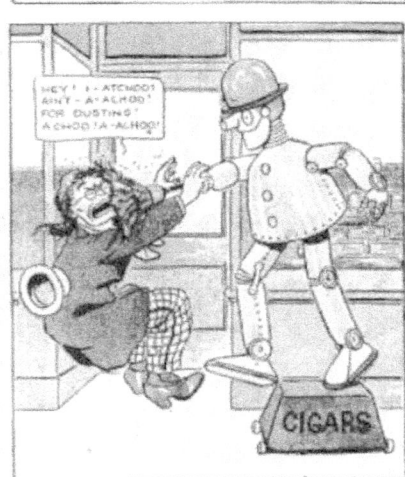
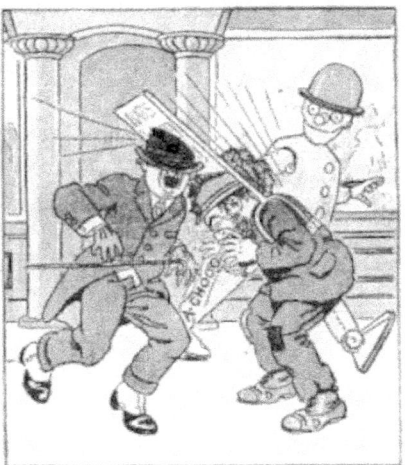

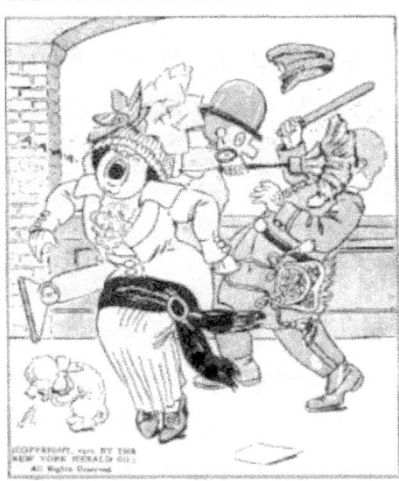
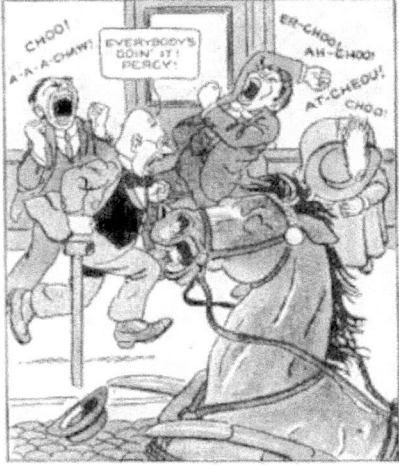
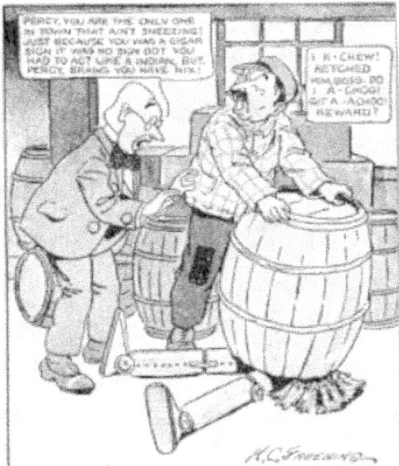

Percy: Brains He Has Nix by Harry Cornell Greening / Comic Strip #60 / Published in the Washington Evening Star November 10, 1912

67

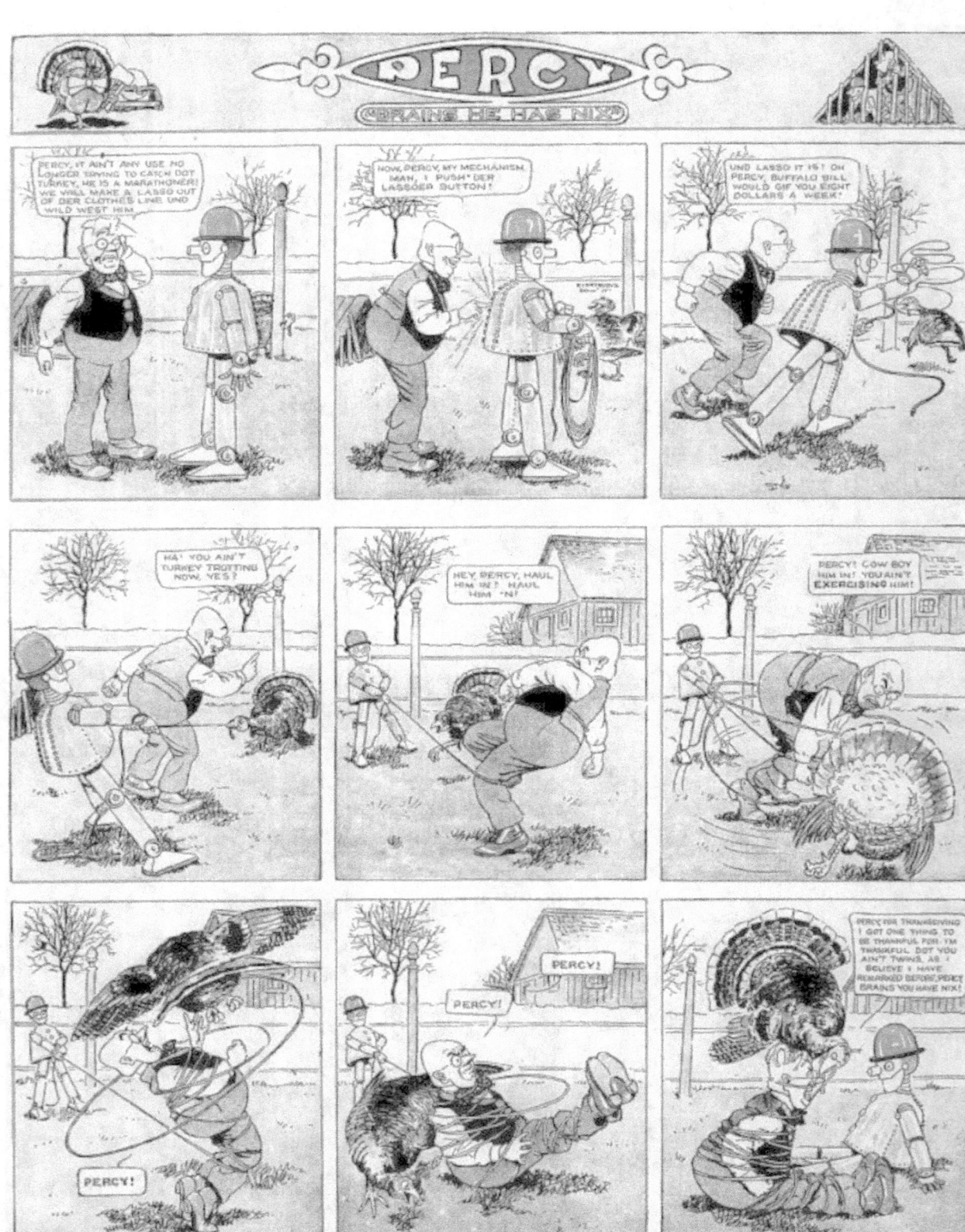

Percy: Brains He Has Nix by Harry Cornell Greening / Comic Strip #61 / Published in the Washington Evening Star November 17, 1912

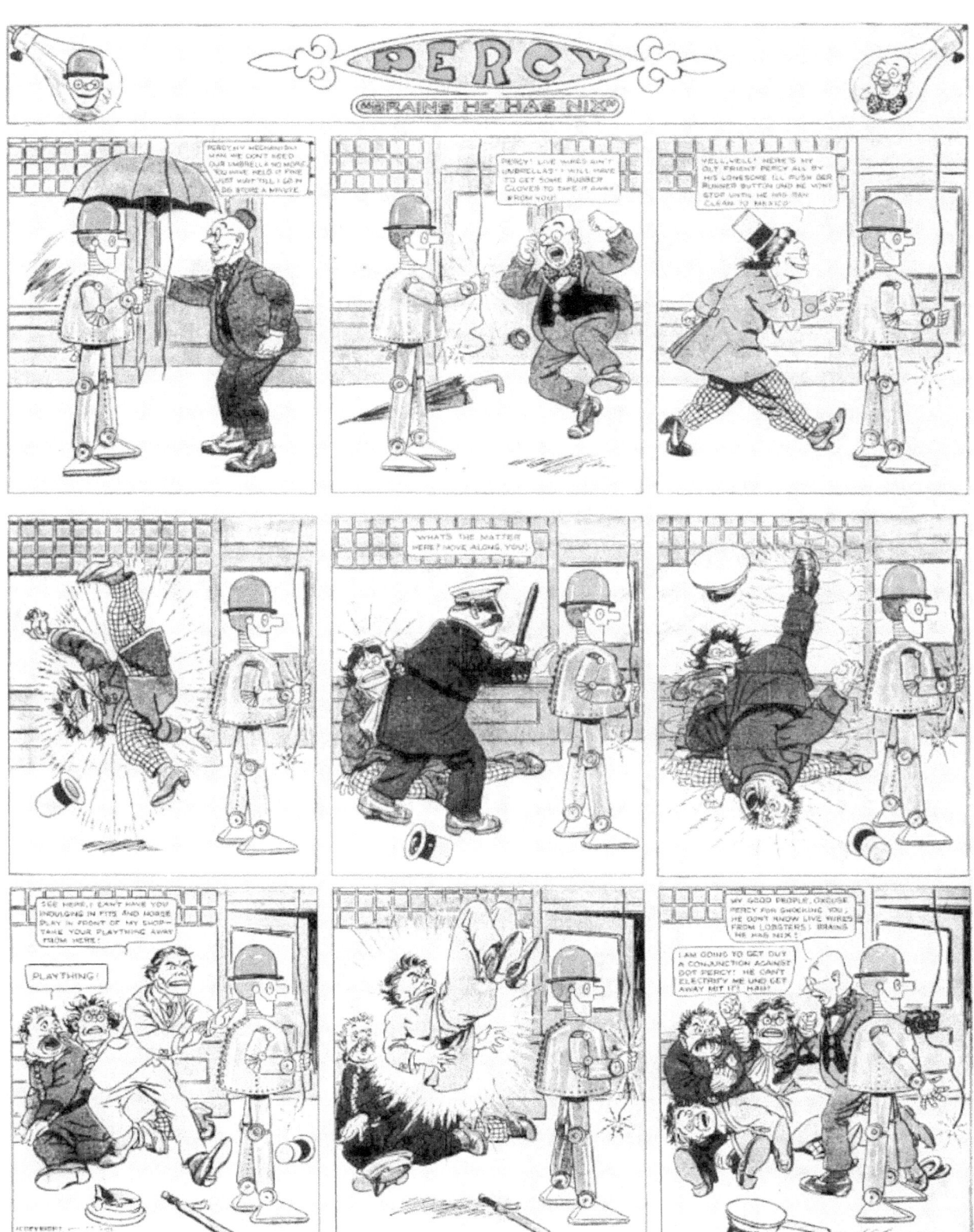

Percy: Brains He Has Nix by Harry Cornell Greening / Comic Strip #62 / Published in the Washington Evening Star November 24, 1912

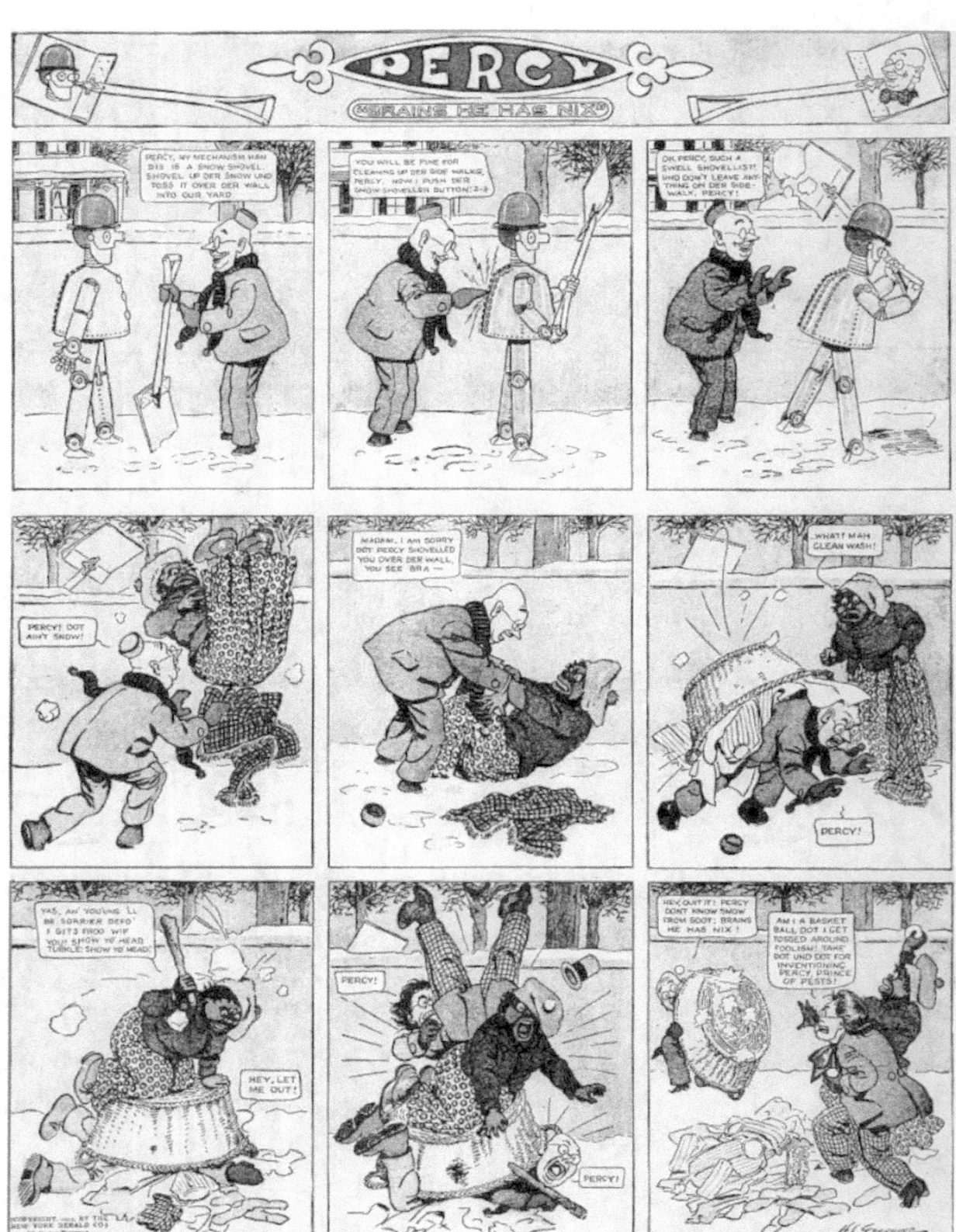

Percy: Brains He Has Nix by Harry Cornell Greening / Comic Strip #63 / Published in the Washington Evening Star December 1, 1912

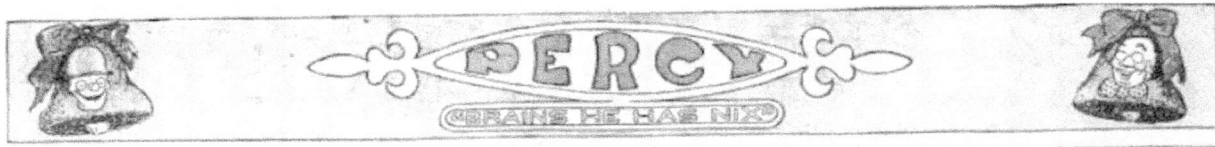

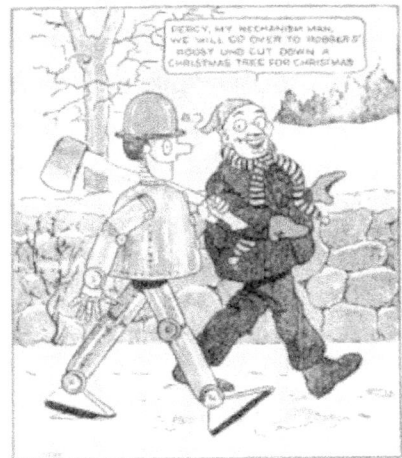
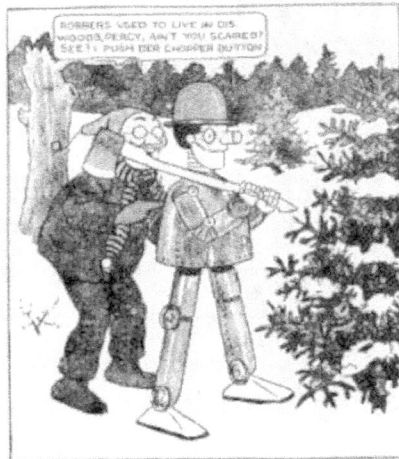
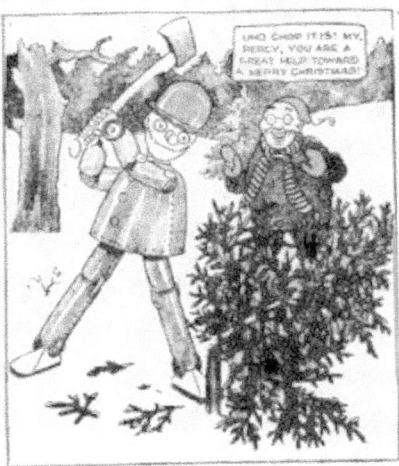

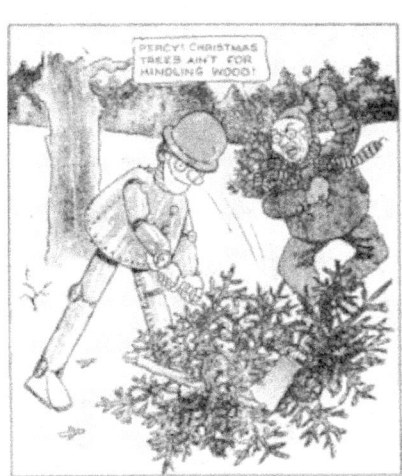
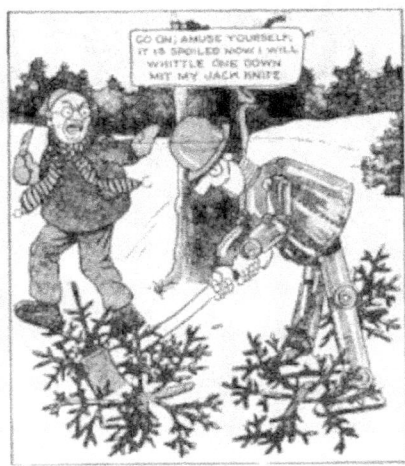
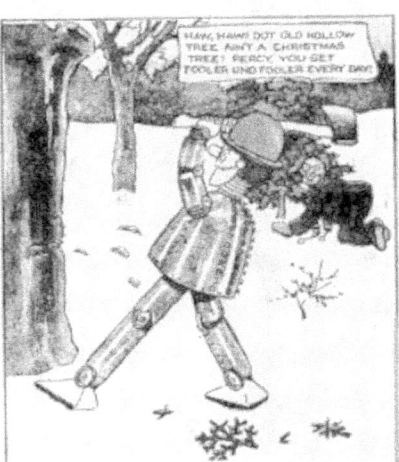

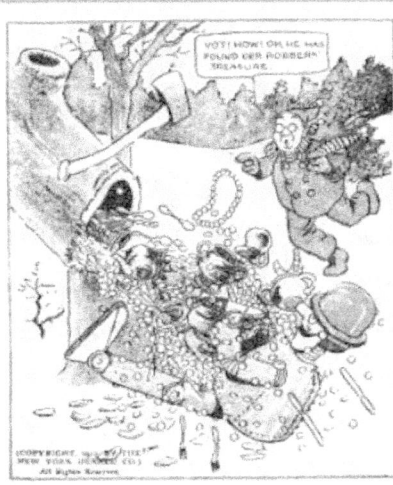
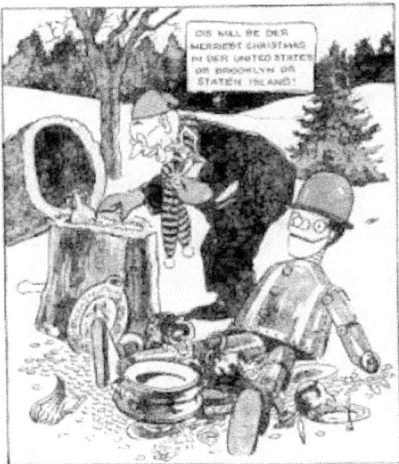
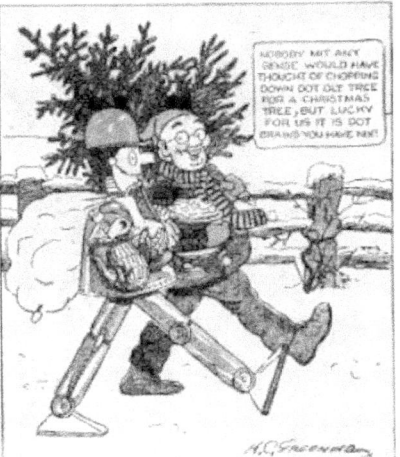

Percy: Brains He Has Nix by Harry Cornell Greening / Comic Strip #64 / Published in the Washington Evening Star December 8, 1912

71

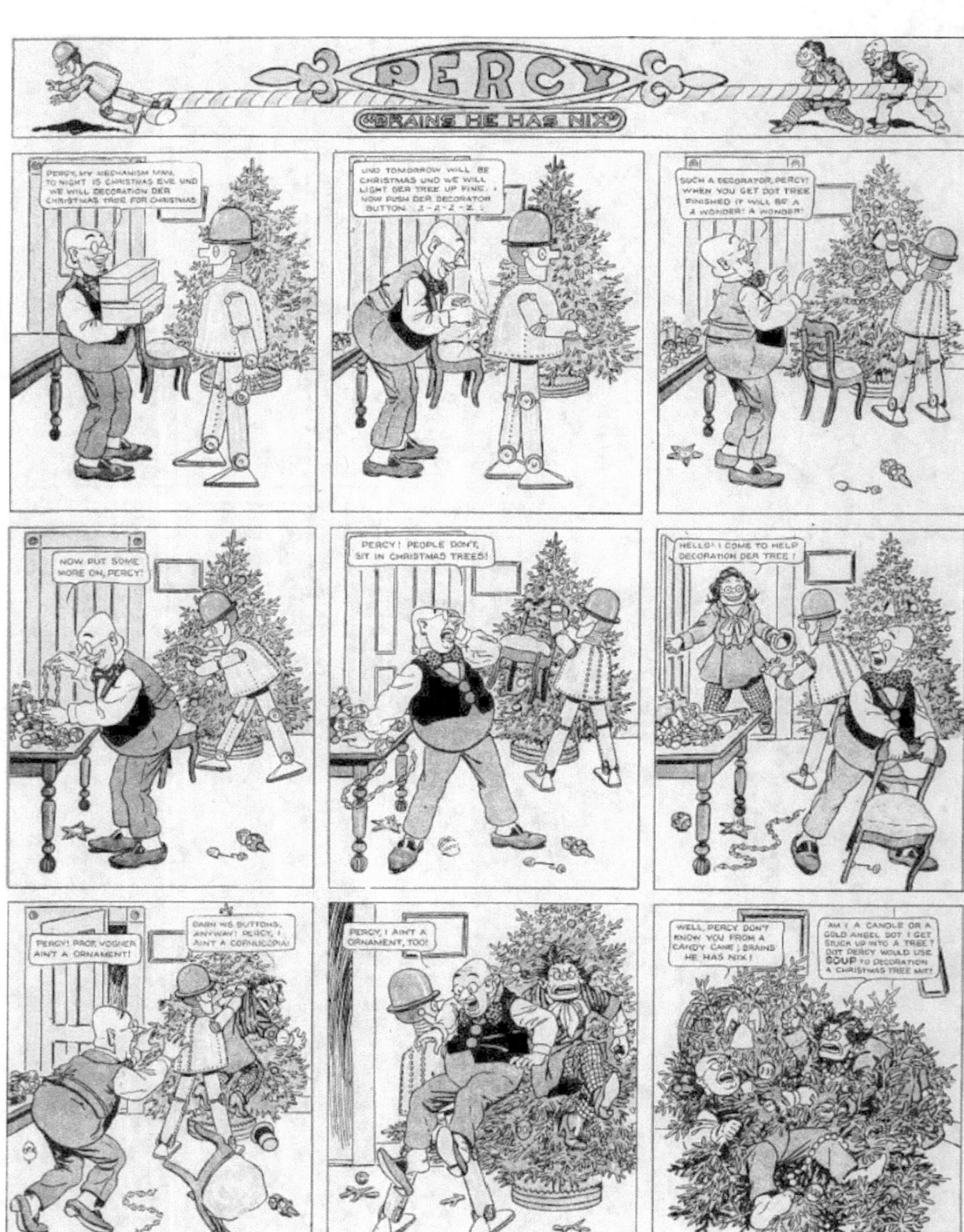

Percy: Brains He Has Nix by Harry Cornell Greening / Comic Strip #65 / Published in the Washington Evening Star December 15, 1912

72

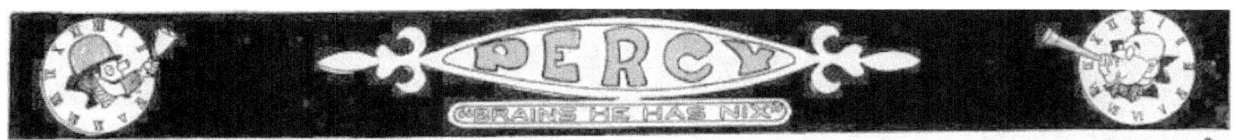

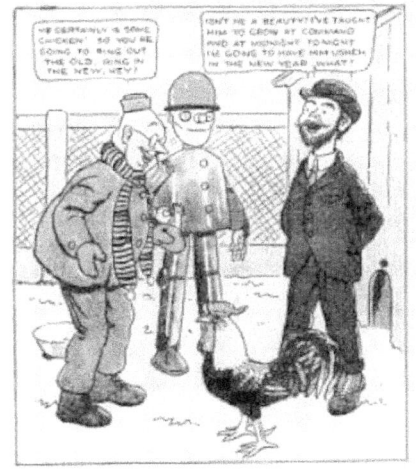 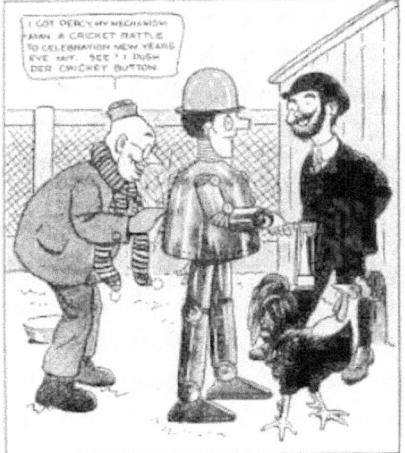 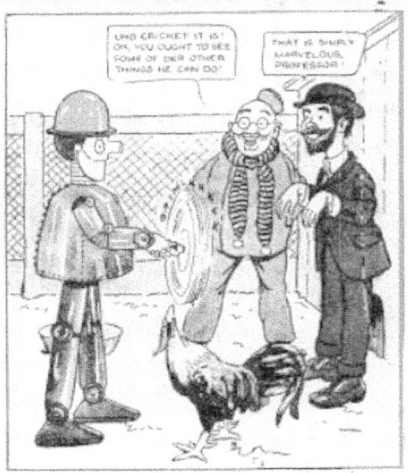

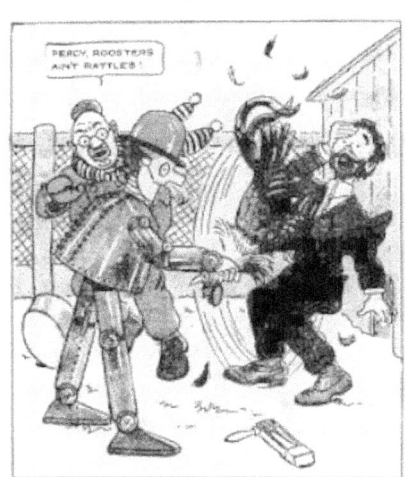 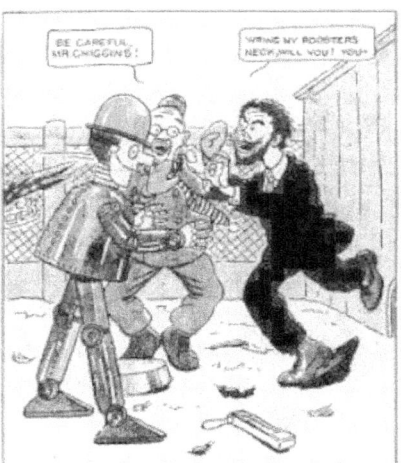 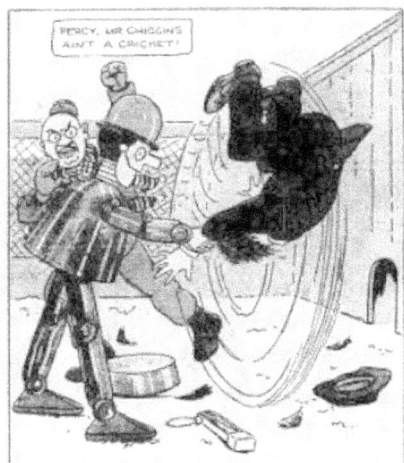

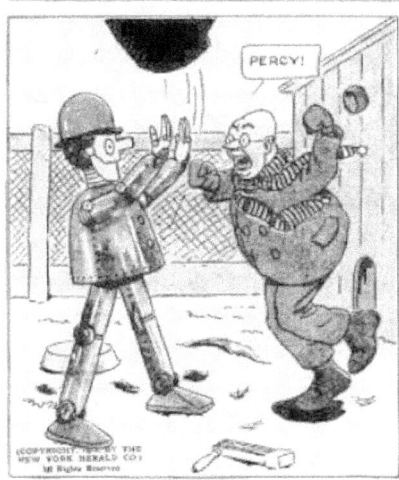 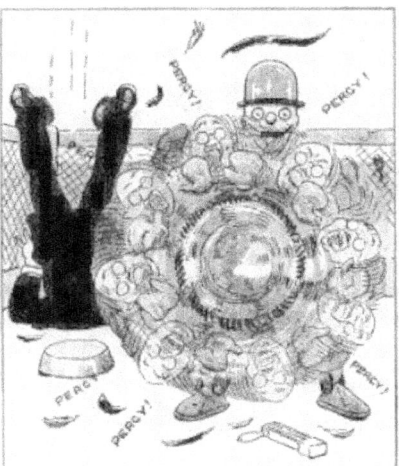 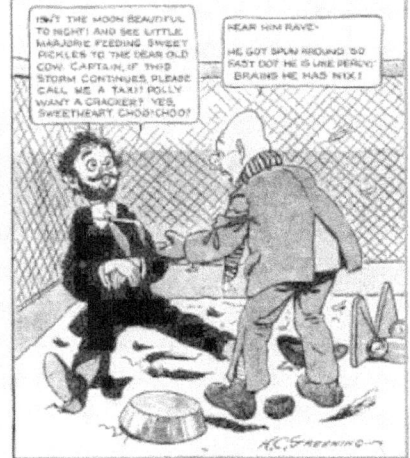

Percy: Brains He Has Nix by Harry Cornell Greening / Comic Strip #66 / Published in the Washington Evening Star December 22, 1912

73

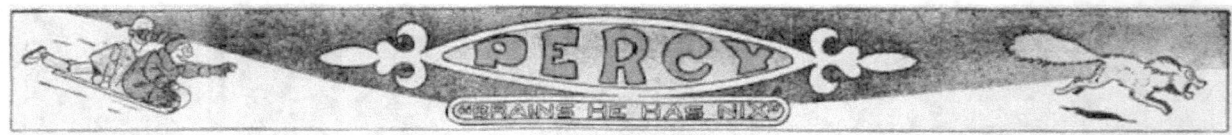

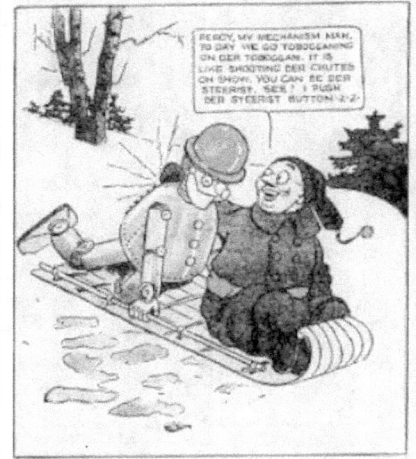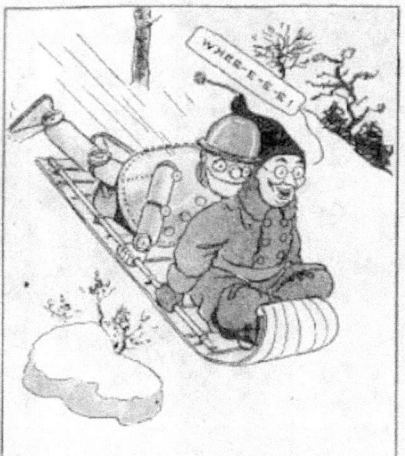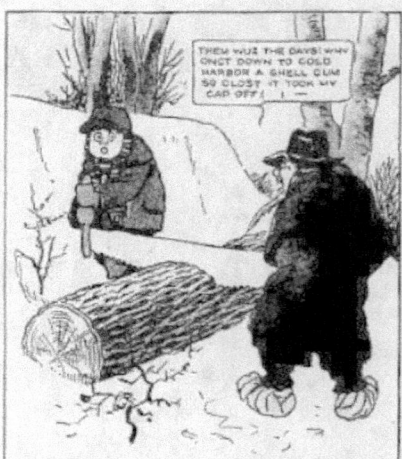

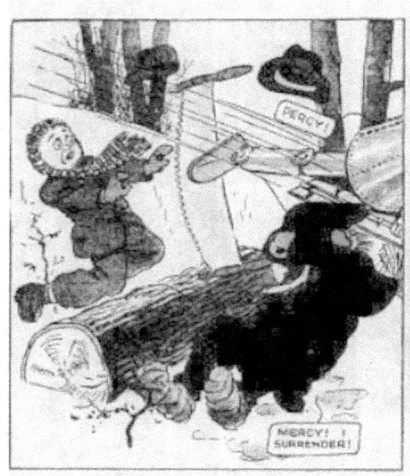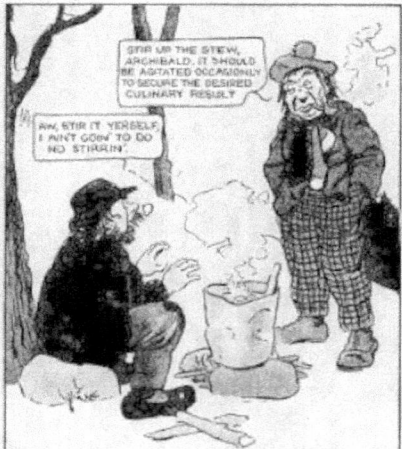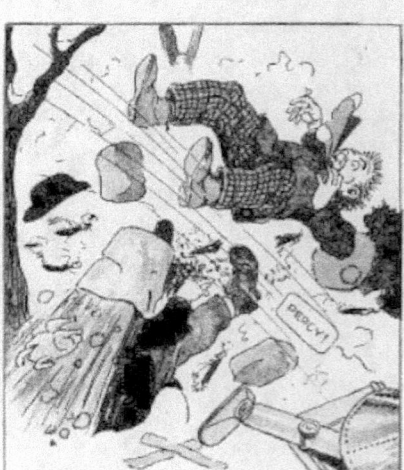

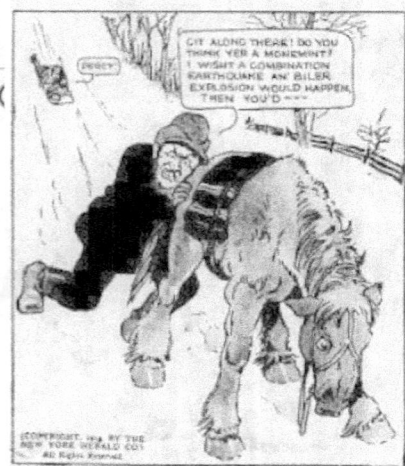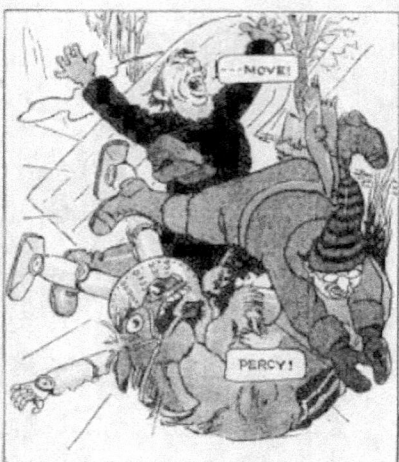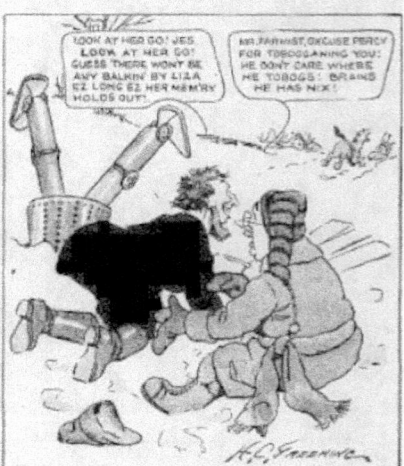

Percy: Brains He Has Nix by Harry Cornell Greening / Comic Strip #67 / Published in the Washington Evening Star January 5, 1913

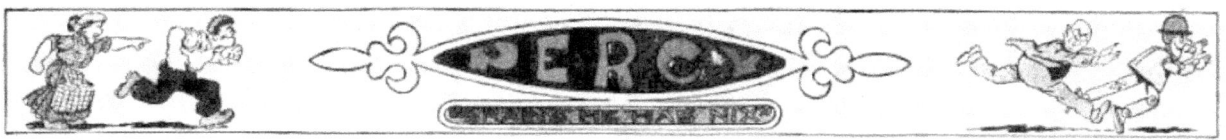

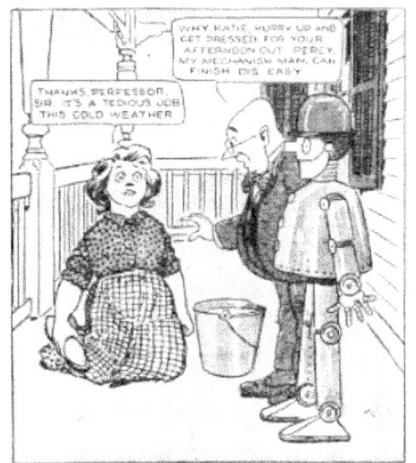 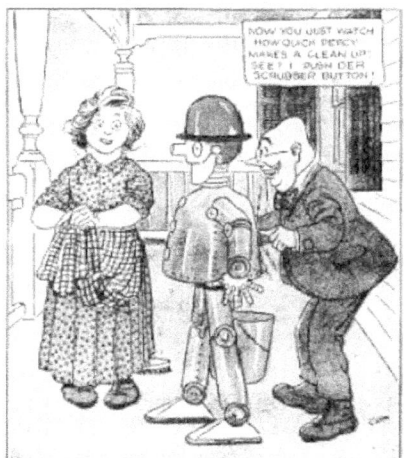 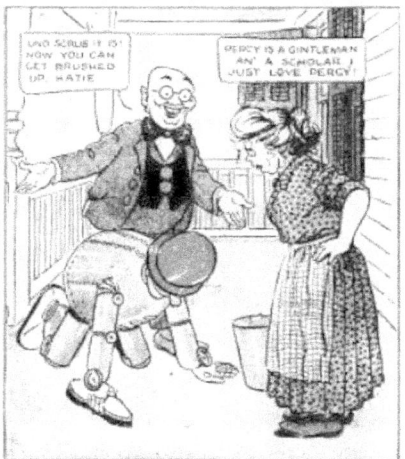

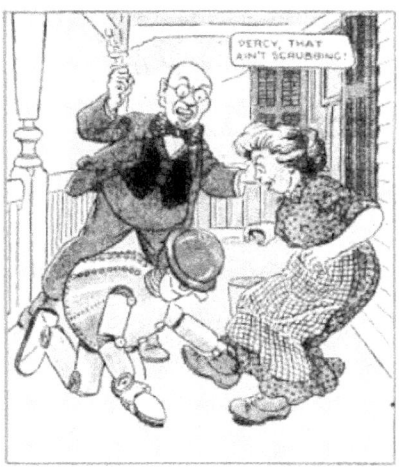 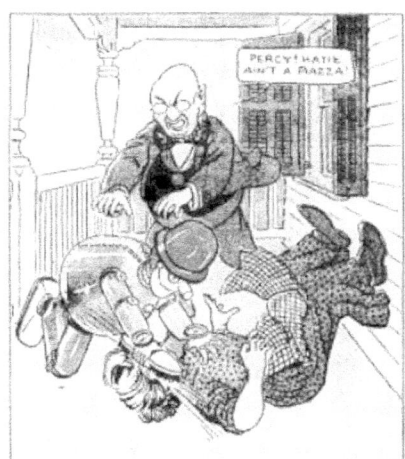 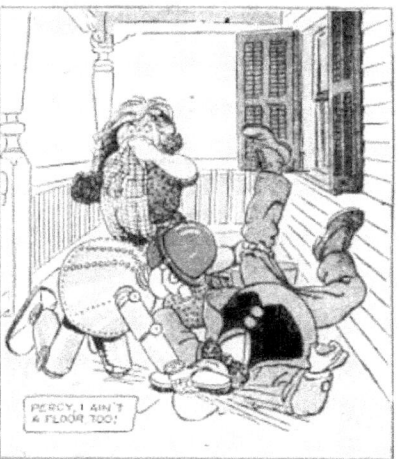

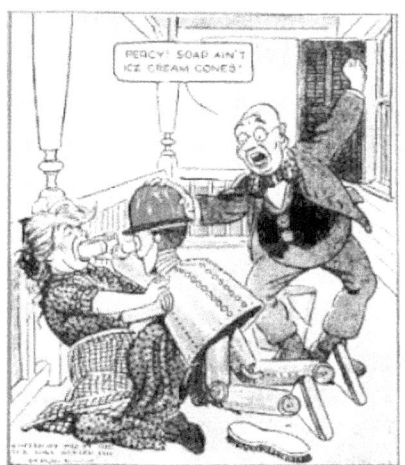 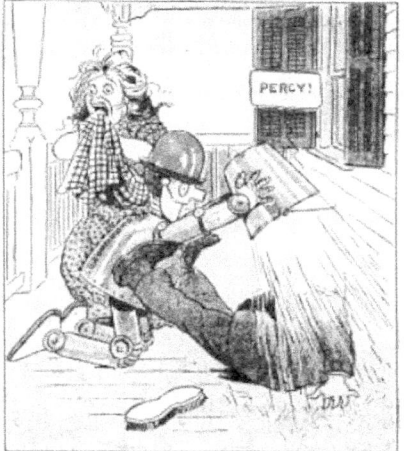 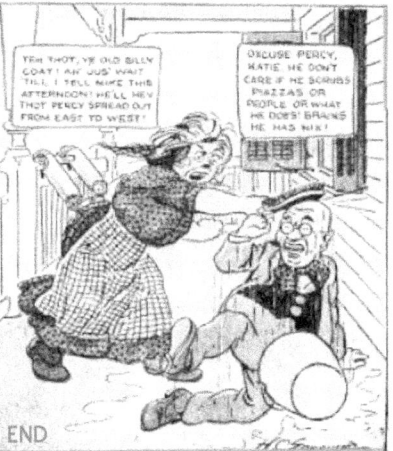

Percy: Brains He Has Nix by Harry Cornell Greening / Comic Strip #68 / Published in the Washington Evening Star January 13, 1913

The
End

www.ingramcontent.com/pod-product-compliance
Lightning Source LLC
Chambersburg PA
CBHW060001230526
45472CB00008B/1895